Where I Belong

*Overcoming Bipolar Disorder and Its Stigma
through the Love of Jesus Christ*

Kristi Kay Price

Copyright 2024 by Kristi Kay Price

Published by Electric Moon Publishing, LLC

©2024 *Where I Belong: Overcoming the Stigma of Bipolar Disorder through the Love of Jesus Christ* / Kristi Kay Price

Paperback ISBN: 978-1-943027-75-0
E-book ISBN: 978-1-943027-76-7

Electric Moon Publishing, LLC
P.O. Box 466
Stromsburg, NE 68666
info@emoonpublishing.com

All scripture notations are taken from Holy Bible, New International Version®, NIV® Copyright ©1973, 1978, 1984, 2011 by Biblica, Inc.® Used by permission. All rights reserved worldwide.

NOTE TO READER: *To the best of my ability I have re-created events, locales, people, and organizations from my memories of them. In order to maintain the anonymity of others, in some instances I have changed the names of individuals and places and the details of events. I have also changed some identifying characteristics, such as physical descriptions, occupations, and places of residence. Sensitive topics are discussed. Reader discretion is advised.*
—*Kristi Kay Price*

All rights reserved. No part of this publication may be reproduced, distributed, or transmitted in any form or by any means, including photocopying, recording, or other electronic or mechanical methods, without the prior written permission of the publisher, except in the case of brief quotations embodied in critical reviews and certain other noncommercial uses permitted by copyright law. For permission requests, write to the publisher.

The opinions and quotations of the author are not necessarily that of the publisher or its affiliates. Author retains all intellectual property rights. Contact author for questions.

All website addresses listed herein are accurate at the time of publication but may change in the future or cease to exist. The listing of website references and resources does not imply publisher/author endorsement of the site's entire contents. Groups, corporations, and organizations are listed for informational purposes, and listing does not imply publisher/author endorsement of activities.

Cover and Interior Design by Lyn Rayn / Electric Moon Publishing Creative Services

Printed in the United States of America

www.emoonpublishing.com

Dedicated to the **One** who is always there,
and to the **one** who needs that reminder.

IN MEMORIAM

In loving memory of my father, Kenneth Clair Price, who often whispered, "Heaven is the most beautiful place I could ever imagine." He went home to be with the Lord on June 15, 2022, after battling Alzheimer's disease.

Contents

Prologue	9
1. Little Girl Lost	13
2. Teenage Girl Lost and Found	21
3. Passion for Fashion	29
4. The Love of a Family	37
5. The Diagnosis	53
6. Bipolar Meets God	69
7. Ending a Marriage	75
8. New Beginnings	83
9. Hope for a Melancholy Heart	105
10. Days of Promise	119
11. From Darkness to Light	129
Testimonies of Faith	143
Songspiration	145
Acknowledgments	147
About the Author	151
Parting Thoughts	153

PROLOGUE

With God

We know that in all things God works for the good of those who love him.
—Romans 8:28

"Oh, Lord, you're beautiful."
—Keith Green

A radio plays in the background while I snuggle on the sofa with a favorite blanket. The lyrics of a song settle over me–welcoming and peaceful. God's love is unconditional, and the desire to sit in His presence is extraordinary.

Folding my hands, I bow my forehead against them, breathe deeply, and enjoy a moment with the Lord. When my older son, Michael, walks in, I ask him to take a picture. I want to remember this.

Of course, not all memories are picture-perfect, are they?

Many times I had to find my way back to God—particularly after receiving a diagnosis of bipolar disorder. The depression proved unmanageable for years, and generally I didn't seek God or pray as I was taught to do. Part of me gave up on God, and then I gave up on myself.

Prologue

And when I did try, my prayers sounded like cries for help: *Lord, where are you? I need you! Can't you hear me? Don't you love me anymore?* On one hand I didn't even expect an answer, but on the other I couldn't understand why God would abandon me.

During one particular depressive episode and seeking respite, I visited my father and stepmother. We went shopping one day and stepped into a thrift store. As I walked the aisles, a framed copy of "Footprints in the Sand" caught my eye. My childhood bedroom had a framed copy too. I cried.

At that moment I realized that God had never left my side. Never. Not during the worst episodes of depression nor in any other dark situation. Even when I thought He had abandoned me, never once had God left me alone. Rather, He had carried me just as He had the poem's dreaming man.

The memory brings me back to the here and now—on the couch, under my blanket. That poem always meant a lot to me, and I carry its meaning still.

Again I bow my head—silent. *Thank you, Heavenly Father, for the gift of life and for being with me every moment. I have made mistakes. I know I have failed you time and time again. Please forgive my shortcomings and help me continue to overcome the darkness, for you know it's a daily struggle for me. I desperately need the reminder that I am loved. Amen.*

Deep inside, all I ever wanted was to fit in and just be me. It would take years to accomplish with many obstacles to overcome. But through the struggles, I came to accept Jesus Christ fully.

Were it not for the depression and the hurt, I would not have fallen so low as to need to look up and ask for His help. In that painful place I reached out and asked His forgiveness. I drew near to God, and He drew near to me.

"Wonderful, Merciful Savior." The lyrics of that song run through my head and reach deeply inside. Only God had granted me mercy.

Only God had brought peace to my heart. Only God had been able to rescue me.

On my couch I remember the moment and remember to be intentional with God now—every day—not to take His presence for granted and then miss His presence altogether. So under the blanket I bring all my burdens to Him once again. And as the radio plays, it's as if God says to me, "It is going to be okay."

"Oh, Lord, You're Beautiful" finishes playing just then. God was speaking through the lyrics—an intimate moment that I would never forget.

Loving, inspiring and reassuring, the Spirit awakens my melancholy heart. Time to trust, time to heal and fully surrender to God. Suffocating in the darkness, I whisper, "Lord, help me to breathe. I want to feel alive again."

Then comes a sense of peace and the realization that life isn't all about me. God calls us to be brave and share our light with the world. By helping others, I can heal and be part of the ordinary world. As the fear subsides, hope remains. It isn't all bad! There are happy things going on in my life in spite of the struggles.

Like a sponge, I soak up the moment, unable to get enough of God and His love. My mind clears from the clutter of depression and darkness. I welcome the light and breathe in serenity.

Part of my story is about bipolar disorder: the diagnosis, the symptoms, the struggles. But it's also about my journey with God and spiritual transformation—overcoming the darkness and shining in the light. This book is about both.

CHAPTER 1

Little Girl Lost

*She is clothed with strength and dignity;
she can laugh at the days to come.*
—Proverbs 31:25

"I will follow."
—Chris Tomlin

My eyes graze the keyboard as I write, amid the cozy chaos that is my desk. Photos, figurines, sticky notes, and memes. Maybe even a half-eaten peanut butter sandwich.

Also on my desk, a Bible. I look at it and remember my solid Christian upbringing. I was one of three children in a typical middle-class Midwestern family. Every Sunday without fail we attended Sunday School and worship service and were involved in many activities. Church was a familiar and safe place and gave me a sense of belonging. My parents planted the seed of how important God was in everyday life.

I *am* a child of God. I knew very young that He loved me unconditionally just the way I was. My foundation in Him was unbreakable. He would never love me any differently throughout my life—always there in spirit, always there to whisper to and always there to lean on in tough times.

That same little girl looks back at me from a photo on my desk—tidy and petite, in a green dress and short muffin hairdo. God knew my name and made me in His image. Kristi Kay was flawless in His eyes. I was innocent and carefree—this picture is a reminder of when I was content. This little girl skipped to school, laughed in the classroom, and was confident and happy-go-lucky. That was about to change.

After seeing an eye doctor in the second grade, I was prescribed my first pair of glasses. Round pop-bottle glasses covered my tiny face and altered my appearance. The schoolboys noticed. They were particularly mean, barking at me and branding me as a dog. The teasing continued all through my grade school years. Obviously I didn't fit in with the other students, even the girls.

On the playground the popular girls would congregate on the merry-go-round, protecting their space from others while flaunting beautiful long hair and pretty faces. Being shunned by the group, I made my way to the swing set to rock alone. Looking up, I whispered, "God, why didn't you make *me* pretty?"

Classmates knew Kristi Kay as habitually awkward, timid, and weak. *I* was the girl who sat alone in the cafeteria. *I* was the clumsy girl who tripped over her own two feet, and *I* was the girl picked last during dodgeball. Humiliated and rejected, I couldn't understand why the other kids didn't like me because I was *also* the imaginative, even-tempered girl who was kind to everyone. Kristi Kay stopped seeing life through big, wide eyes. Instead, the world dimmed, and she began fading away into loneliness. I was *just* a little girl, but Kristi Kay became "Little Girl Lost."

Sitting at my desk, I remember those lonely feelings. No one seemed to notice me—for anything good anyway. This went on for years without relief. No one else really understood, so I developed ways of coping. *Alone* was a safe place.

That summer my family moved to a brand-new home in the country, where I could just be myself. A mile past town sat the new house—a place of promise and grand adventure. The acreage became a place of respite from the "somebodies" at school. I was able to roam free, and I had kittens as playmates. They loved hearing my stories and would snuggle with me when I felt lonely.

Besides having a new house, our acreage also had a barn. Parked against it were an old Rambler and a Falcon. And inside was a wood-burning stove where we could enjoy freshly popped popcorn. This was my dad's hangout place, and often I would join him for an afternoon snack. It was a special place—cozy, loving, and familiar.

Around the perimeter of our eight acres was a homemade track and weathered go-kart. Although I had to share it with my siblings, there was plenty of time to sit back and enjoy the ride. With not a care in the world, I made endless laps on my "courage-mobile." Being brave felt good, so I took the turns a little faster and even went airborne when no one was watching. Laughing was one way for me to let go of my worries and smile. Kristi Kay was fearless and full of fire.

Inside the brick home was my childhood bedroom with my desk, a pile of freshly laundered clothes folded in a stack on the floor, and a basket of dolls. One in particular was a cheap knock-off Barbie from the five-and-dime store. Was I not good enough to have a real one? In disgust, I cut her hair while holding her in my hand and wondered if she felt ugly and lonely too. Neither one of us would ever be worthy.

Those were lonely years. Even my parents, it seemed, gave most of their attention to my sister and brother. I was the classic middle child. And at school, I was compared to my siblings, too.

Why not run away with my kitten and my doll? My canteen and fruit roll-ups could go in my backpack, and a friend's farm was just a few miles down the road. I knew the way, and walking briskly, I could make it in a few hours. The journey would be easy—I would disappear without leaving a note since I was the "invisible" child.

All of a sudden, panic set in. What about the big dog along the way? Cujo guarded the driveway two miles south. No one made it past without a chase.

So much for that idea. I couldn't even run away.

Defeated, I felt trapped. Whether at home or at school, I began putting up imaginary walls. If no one could get in, no one could hurt me.

Then, when I was in fifth grade, something surprising happened. Our teacher let us share show-and-tell stories in preparation for creative writing. I was excited to share my ideas in writing, of which there were many. There was something magical about a blank notebook and strawberry-scented pencil. Imagination flowed, and expressing my thoughts came naturally. Creating fictional stories was a newfound way of escaping reality. But maybe it was a positive way.

Sixth grade brought a new girl to school, and she noticed *me*. Her name was Ginny, and she was my first true friend. She wore pop-bottle glasses like mine and donned a girly mullet and crooked smile—we connected instantly. Finally, Kristi Kay had someone to eat lunch with, talk to, and swing with on the playground.

Both of us wanted to meet new friends, so Ginny's mom hosted a slumber party, which would begin Friday after school.

The sleepover started at Skate World with six giggly girls. We laced up our skates tightly and then entered the rink, skating perfectly to capture the attention of numerous boys. A hand-in-hand trip around the rink with a boy was a highly prized goal among the girls.

My new friends and I skated together to form a line when "Downtown" played through the speakers at the end of the evening. This was a contest. The loudest group would receive free drinks and nachos at the snack bar. With no serious competition coming close, the six of us won!

At home, after changing into our fancy pajamas and slippers, we wrapped up in cozy blankets, snacking on popcorn and Diet Coke while watching a couple Brat Pack movies. We couldn't stop laughing when we realized how much my sister resembled Molly Ringwald as we watched *Pretty in Pink*. And who could forget Anthony Michael Hall from *Sixteen Candles*? The movies—perfect. We were all coming of age and had so much to talk about. Good thing we had all night.

In Ginny's room a purple bedspread and curtains matched perfectly. On the vanity were a stack of jelly bracelets, bottles of perfume, and a caddy full of nail polish in every color. Tucked behind a stack of books was Ginny's diary, full of secrets.

Nearby was a dresser with a gigantic boom box on top. Now the party was really starting. With the music blaring as loudly as it could go, we sang along with our makeshift microphones as if we were rock stars. Didn't every girl dream of stardom?

Finally, giving up on our singing careers after 2:00 a.m., we all sat on the bed together. We talked about the latest fashions in *Teen Magazine*, the poster on the wall of the dreamy Kirk Cameron, and giggled about the cute boys at school. We were indeed starting to notice boys. After all, in just a few short weeks we wouldn't be in grade school anymore. With those final thoughts we drifted to sleep.

Next morning, the fun continued as we walked downtown for donuts. I had such a newfound sense of belonging. Feeling confident, I asked what *we* were going to do over the summer. That's when Ginny suggested a swim team, and she invited me to join.

The pool was a perfect fit. It was my favorite place in the summer, and I was an excellent swimmer, so good in fact that I helped with swimming lessons. After lunch I would return until the pool closed that evening. All the lifeguards knew me well.

Dark overcast days were the best since attendance was low

Where I Belong

then and I had the pool mostly all to myself. Swimming laps all afternoon cleared my mind. There was something magical about gliding through the water. The repetitive motion naturally calmed my anxiety.

Little did I know, the pool manager noticed my perfect swim form and vigorous movements. She complimented me and encouraged me in my efforts to improve. That was good advice since I wanted to impress the popular girls on the swim team. Maybe they would accept me if I were successful. But I would have to work hard.

Swim team practice started at 7:00 a.m. every morning. The coaches welcomed me and a few others as new members. By the third day, new friendships were formed, and I seemed to fit in. I was in my element. After the very first meeting everyone saw how strong I was. Spectators, coaches, and teammates cheered me on during competitions. No one was surprised when the coaches presented me with my first ribbons and medals.

At the annual relay meet, I was teamed up with three other girls. Anxiety set in for a moment, but I took my stance at the starting block and dove into the water the moment my teammate reached the wall. Pulling ahead, swimming breaststroke, I won the relay for my team. As I got out of the water, popular girls patted me on the back and chanted my name, *Kristi, Kristi!* They had never talked to me before. This girl was on fire.

But three days later the team welcomed even more kids, including my younger brother. He was tall, fast, and swam all four strokes with perfection. Instantly he was a champion swimmer, and all eyes were on him. He stole the spotlight. It was silly of me to think the glory could last forever.

Despite being a champion swimmer myself, the popular girls now shunned me—just as they had on the merry-go-round so long ago. At the pool they protected their space as I walked over to join them. Their stares said it all, and it hurt.

Knowing I wasn't welcome, I laid down my towel and jumped into the pool. It was far easier to swim laps all day than to sit on the deck alone. I was closing off again, and the imaginary walls went back up. To be accepted was all I ever wanted, but my spirit broke, and once again Kristi Kay was "Little Girl Lost."

CHAPTER 2

Teenage Girl Lost and Found

*For by grace you have been saved through faith.
And this is not your own doing; it is the gift of God.*
—Ephesians 2:8

"Who am I?"
—Casting Crowns

On a crisp morning, coffee in hand, I stroll out the door of my bungalow to grab the mail. Fall is in the air, and I'm taken aback by its beauty—trees changing color, pumpkins dotting the neighborhood, and leaves falling onto the brick walkway, so many, in fact, that I hear the repeated crunch under my feet.

To my delight, there is an envelope from my alma mater in the mailbox. I head back to the porch swing, invitation in hand. It's a class reunion. I'm flooded with memories and mixed emotions over fall seasons long ago and the school auditorium—a symbolic place of being lost and yet finding myself again despite the bumps along the way.

Every day of junior high and high school began in the auditorium. Most of us sat in the wooden theater chairs, eyes focused on the stage.

But of course, that's where the "pops" would gather and sit with their legs dangling off the edge.

They wore name-brand clothes from the strip mall, and I sat in unbranded jeans and a top from Kmart. If I didn't look like them, I would never fit in. I couldn't wait for the sound of the bell to rescue me.

After lunch, it was back to the auditorium and I would again sit in one of the wooden theater chairs, looking at the stage, where I didn't belong. Pretty girls on one end, boys on the other, flirting back and forth. It wasn't fair. The pretty girls had everything—popularity, clothes, and even the boys. No matter where I went, there was always a reminder of "Little Girl Lost."

My clique hung out in the basement band room. As classic band geeks, this is where *we* ruled. With lots of laughter and joyful noises, it was a safe atmosphere. My bandmates shared the same passion for music—a silent code between us of unity, understanding, and acceptance.

Playing the clarinet came naturally from the first time my lips touched the mouthpiece. I played with gusto, and the band teacher noticed. He encouraged me to practice often for all the upcoming events. I didn't mind the extra effort, be it playing alone at home or in the band room with friends. Music offered relief from the anxiety and clutter in my mind.

The most important event to me was the concert band in the auditorium. I walked the stage steps proudly and sat with my bass clarinet. With the wave of the director's baton, the music began, and after a grand performance we took our final bow. Kristi Kay was on the *stage* and now she belonged there. "Little Girl Lost" was on her way to being found, but there would be another obstacle.

Back on the porch sipping coffee, I hear church bells down the street. I have so many good memories of church as I was growing up here, but they weren't all happy.

Church was the one place I was supposed to feel safe and free of being shunned. However, our three-month confirmation class consisted of two pretty girls and two cute boys—including the one who had branded me a dog. Fortunately, two fellow loners were also in the class, and we banded together.

Wednesday night classes seemed to last forever, but most difficult was the all-day retreat. Even though I had my two friends to sit with at the back of the bus, it still wasn't fun being shunned by the rest of the group.

And when confirmation day came in May, I stood in front of the church surrounded by the very ones who had ignored me. In my white dress and pink shoes, I held back the tears. No one knew. Silently looking up to the Lord, I cried out, "God, why don't they like me? Why don't I fit in? Will I ever be *a someone*?" Maybe God heard my prayer, because something good was on the way.

I did have a few school friends and we were inseparable. We would walk downtown and mingle or just hang out like any other eighth-grade group of girls. And when cheer tryouts were announced, we decided to go for it. Every day we practiced diligently. We had to be perfect to make the cut. Every jump, every yell, and every clap would be judged and voted on by the seventh- and eighth-grade student body in the auditorium.

When tryout day arrived, my friends and I took the stage and gave the performance of a lifetime. Cheering and clapping nourished my soul, much like the praise I received from the swim team and band. I loved being in front of an audience, and I beamed with confidence.

Moments later a "pop" from the high school cheerleading squad ran over and hugged me with great news. I had made the high school cheerleading team! I was ecstatic. Gone were the days of being anxious. Gone were the days of not belonging. "Teenage girl lost" had become "teenage girl found"—for a while anyway.

In a small town it's easy to hear the school's marching band on fall mornings. High school—oh, the memories! I flip through my yearbooks on the porch swing and get a few butterflies. Those years carry a mixed bag of emotions. Walking into the gymnasium as a freshman—seems like it happened yesterday, as does wearing my cap and gown at the end of my senior year.

That first day started with the freshmen huddled in their hallway and the sound of locker doors slamming as students scurried off to their first class. Then at lunchtime we grabbed our favorite octagon-shaped Mexican pizza and a little gossip before the next period and waited for the day's final bell. After school it was time for cross-country and a two-mile run. Then finally cheer practice—time with my close friends.

Game days were the best—full of school colors and school spirit, and in the gym a pep rally led by the cheerleaders. When the school song ended and the final bell sounded, we went to the Dairy Chef for a quick bite to eat. It was *the* place to be before the game.

As they say, "Friday night lights!" On the field, the toss of the football snapped before a roaring crowd. Poms in hand, we cheered and the pep band played, hoping to celebrate later in the parking lot. These were among my happiest memories as the days flew by.

As a sophomore I ran my second and final race at the state cross-country meet and turned sixteen a week later. We celebrated by piling into my burnt-orange Chevette for the first of many cruises. Hanging out strengthened our bond and made me realize just how precious friends were. I couldn't wait for summer.

Weekend sleepovers were a must! We formed sister-like bonds and looked forward to the time together. We spread our pillows and blankets on the floor and gossiped about girly stuff—the latest hairstyles, clothes, and the cutest boy in school.

At the breakfast nook we indulged in leftover pizza and diet soda while we registered for cheerleading camp. A few days later we drove to the strip mall in the city, where we bought outfits for camp.

On the first day of cheerleading camp, as we settled into the dorm rooms, the radio played in the background. The DJ for the local station gave a warm welcome and declared a contest. The first cheerleader to call would talk on the air and announce the hit song live! I won! Everyone heard *my* voice. It was an exciting moment. And more fun was to come—for a little while anyway.

Later that afternoon we walked a few blocks to the football stadium. On the field professional cheerleaders taught each squad new cheers and dance routines. For the next four days hundreds of girls shouted, kicked, and jumped in unison—even a few cartwheels for show.

On the last day, the grand performance, we *hipped 'n' shaked* to the blaring music. Standing proudly on the field with the girls, I realized that popularity had a new meaning—*acceptance* and *belonging*. Camp ended in a camera pose with the hot camp leader. Every girl swooned over him, including me.

It was time to go home. Polaroids in hand, we giggled as we drove, with confidence and maturity and photos that would never be forgotten. The miles flew by and our energy waned. Conversation and talk turned into summer plans. For me, summer meant the pool.

At the pool the new season was off to a great start. Meets were held on Monday nights, many of which were hosted at home, but other times we traveled by bus to the towns of the opposing teams. Each time we gave it our all and celebrated many victories.

Everyone knew that the pool was my best friend, and there I practiced during the afternoons and evening hours. The coach noticed and encouraged me to stay focused, because the final invitational was only a few weeks away. The entire team counted down to the last Sunday in July.

Hundreds of swimmers made camp at the park adjacent to the pool and waited to be called "on deck" over the loudspeaker. We scuttled into the pool, where we were assigned a heat. The fifty-yard individual breaststroke was up next. This was *the* race I had trained for all season.

We all took our stance at the starting block. When the starting pistol went off I dove into the water, pulling, kicking, and gliding with perfect form and speed and managed to bring home the gold, beating fifty-six other girls. Kristi Kay was on top of the world—and it was only going to get better.

During the last of summer days, the girls and I met downtown for lunch. There a cute guy caught my attention, and within a few days came the first date. The relationship blossomed quickly, and he showered me with affection, expensive gifts, and special date nights.

I felt beautiful in a long pink dress at the Hawaiian luau. People gazed and shared flattering comments about my tiny waist and pretty smile—things I had never been told before. Later, sitting in the driveway at home, my boyfriend gave me a ring and said, "I love you, Kristi." No one ever made me feel that precious—and finally I *belonged* to *someone*. The feeling was priceless.

I was elated while staring at my reflection in the mirror—pretty and *so* skinny in the pink dress. Perfection was important, especially as a senior girl.

The final year of high school was off to a great start. Senior pictures with the photographer provided a delightful experience since it was all about me and captured many strengths. Then I attended the all-state band event with my close friend and bandmate. It was quite an honor to perform center stage at the new theater in the city. And the first of many "lasts" brought mixed emotions. Gone were the days of marching band, homecoming festivities, and football games, but it also meant more time with my besties.

My friends and I gathered at Shelly's house, and on the table were a myriad of photos. Oh, the memories! We reminisced and giggled on and on . . . until someone asked who the fat girl was.

The photo had been taken at cheerleading camp. *I* was the fat girl! Horrified and humiliated, I left and couldn't stop crying. Something was wrong.

Standing at my bedroom mirror, a pudgy, ugly, broken girl appeared in the reflection. My self-esteem—shattered. Something had snapped inside, and I would never be the same. Not ever.

This was the first time I thought about ending my life, and it was the first night that I hurt myself. With a gentle tap, I broke the drinking glass in my hand and thought, *What if?* Then I cut myself.

Blood trickled down my arm, but surprisingly, it felt like relief. The pain I had held in for years was released, and it felt as though I could breathe again. Cutting helped the anxiety. It was like a drug.

Equally so was starving myself. The only things I allowed myself to eat were diet yogurt or baby food. Sometimes I would even skip those. My weight dropped to eighty pounds.

Nevertheless, my mind would always fill back up with clutter—again and again. The pain was too much, but I kept silent. No one would understand, not even my boyfriend.

Snuggling beside him the next day felt good, but then he saw the cuts. And, of course, he panicked. It was all too much to grasp. Needless to say, our relationship ended abruptly that night.

As I drove home, dark thoughts invaded my mind. I lost control of the car and it rolled. A kind passerby stopped and helped me. Deeper depression set in.

A downhill spiral began when I started drinking alcohol. It was a form of self-medication. Instead of a rush like what cutting provided, it numbed the pain—I would do anything not to feel. Passing out and driving under the influence prompted a wake-up call from close friends who shared their concerns of drunken driving. I could have caused an accident or even worse. Embarrassed and ashamed, I prayed about it. God was listening.

A strong Christian woman led the Bible study I attended. Afterward we talked privately because she noticed the sadness in my eyes. Finally I had someone to share my secrets and shame with.

With tears flowing, I let it all out. There was no judgment, only words of encouragement—and it brought a world of hope in my darkness. Upon her invitation, we met weekly to talk about my troubles and God. As I gave my burdens to Him, the healing began.

My faith was growing, and my self-esteem improved each day. All I ever needed was to love myself just as God had made me. Feeling spiritually refreshed, I led senior Sunday at the Methodist church in Syracuse, Nebraska and received much praise. Things were beginning to look up.

At last came graduation day in the gym with a familiar melody playing in the background and classmates walking the stage one last time in caps and gowns. Then spectacular celebrations occurred all over town, and I said my final goodbyes to friends.

And at the end of the day I stood proudly in front of the bedroom mirror, hands raised about my head. Kristi Kay had done it. This teenage girl was found and college bound!

CHAPTER 3

Passion for Fashion

Every day is a fashion show and the world is the runway.
—Anonymous

"Groove is in the heart."
—Deee-Lite

I'm humming in the kitchen while drying the last of the dishes after lunch. There's just enough coffee for an afternoon read in the sitting room. It's quiet and cozy and I stretch out in the recliner with the latest copy of *Harper's Bazaar*. Flipping through its pages takes me back to my college years, when I discovered my many talents, strengths, and a strong sense of belonging.

On Saturday mornings I would grab a donut and head to the family room. No cartoons for me! An episode of *Style with Elsa Klensch* was on CNN! The world of fashion was fascinating. Most girls wanted to be models– oh, but not me! Kristi Kay was going to be the designer at the end of the runway, and I dreamed of attending Parsons School of Design in New York City. But the small-town girl stayed close to home instead and enrolled at a small local college.

Five weeks after my high school graduation, Mom and Dad moved me into the living quarters on campus. Although it was small, it had all the amenities. An associate's degree in fashion merchandising could be earned in just eighteen months. The small business school was a better fit than the crowded university across town.

College life was simple and smooth–only three classes per day and ample time to make friends and fit into the groove on campus. I was anything but the awkward and timid Kristi Kay, only a confident and pretty blonde, well-liked by all—even by the boys. The new sense of belonging made me content and carefree. Walking to class with friends and hanging out over the lunch hour was a must. Never once did we miss our favorite soap opera while enjoying a sandwich in the cafeteria. Then back to the classroom for one more hour. Time after school was spent working part time at the Catholic hospital.

I greeted staff by name throughout the day with a smile. They knew me as fun, respectful, and hard-working. My boss noticed too and offered me extra hours. What college student wouldn't mind extra money? A classmate of mine decided to join the team too.

The start of another six-week module brought new faces to the classroom. A stunning blonde with a Sandra Dee hairdo walked in wearing a black dress, velvet pumps, and a Louis Vuitton satchel bag in her hand—*an authentic Louis Vuitton!* That was impressive. Ms. Pohl was not only our instructor but also the director of fashion. We looked over the syllabus and dug right in with the first assignment—a research paper on the life and career of a fashion designer of our choice.

The campus library was quiet during the afternoon hours. It took hours to comb through stacks of old style magazines in search of articles about costume and fashion designer Bob Mackie. He was my favorite. I had seen his work many times on television. I hit the jackpot (no pun intended) when I came across colorful photographs of his 1991 Las Vegas-inspired collection in *Vogue* magazine, as well as highlights of his career designing for Hollywood stars. Later, in another magazine, more articles of Mackie's work, a wealth of information no less! But my research paper needed pizazz.

Just then, an aha moment! Mackie had just launched his first fragrance and it was being showcased nationwide. That would give my paper something special.

I raced to a department store at the strip mall to interview a petite sales clerk at the fragrance counter. We giggled like school girls as we talked about Mackie and his work. She smiled at me and said, "I like you. You're lighthearted and spirited, just like the perfume." We both laughed at the familiar slogan, but then she added, "Seriously—you should come work here." That day I left not only with the perfume in a keepsake box but also with a grin.

I stayed up past midnight to put the final touches on the paper. Ms. Pohl applauded the extra effort and awarded me an A+ for the assignment. That taste of success gave me confidence to return to the strip mall to apply for a position at the department store, and I got the job.

The marble floors and bright lighting paved the way to "better women's wear," which showcased intricate displays with the finest apparel. As a sales clerk, I catered to a very specific clientele who didn't mind spending lots of money. Kristi Kay was finally part of the fashion world she had longed to be part of.

"Super Saturday" was a special one-day event. Shoppers flooded the entire store. Dazzling them with a plethora of skills came naturally. The register buzzed nonstop, and at the end of the day my sales had climbed to over two thousand dollars! Everyone clapped and cheered at the team meeting three days later. It felt great to be recognized. More success followed.

Evening shifts were often quiet, so there was plenty of time to master the art of folding, organizing, and memorizing every collection. Good thing too, because a tidy woman in her fifties strolled into the department. I showed her my favorite collection, designed by Liz Claiborne, and explained each piece in detail. She was impressed and made a sizable purchase.

Unbeknownst to me, the woman was a secret shopper—who gave a perfect score. The department director gave me a high five—and a raise! The job was really fun, "just playing in clothes," as I always said. It was a favorite pastime both on and off the clock.

Back in the sitting room I stoke the fire and gaze at the mantle—candles, statuaries, and a handmade oil painting. *Elliotte* was my first original design created in high school, and it reminded me of taking the first steps to becoming a fashion designer. With a blank sketchbook and a charcoal pencil in my hand, I made the stick figure come to life, and with a little practice, I mastered the technique of fashion illustration. Drawing them came naturally. Ms. Pohl gave praise for my working with such precision and having the unique ability to create twenty designs in the time it took classmates to do just one. It was a gift and excelling felt wonderful.

During art class my imagination roamed free, just as it had in grade school—but instead of writing, I painted feelings of elation onto the canvas. Peers raved at my almost-childlike artistic work. It was charmingly vivid. I called it *abstract*, which became my signature style.

Later Ms. Pohl had a big announcement: a contest for all art students on campus. Each participant would create a small painting. The winner would receive a special surprise. This was an opportunity for students to shine.

I stayed after class and grabbed a tote of supplies. I played the radio while painting to the beat of the music. Splish, splash, dab, dab, dab. Bright, vibrant colors fell onto the canvas. I also used my fingers against the brush to spackle for texture. To me it felt like a masterpiece!

All the entries were voted on by selected teachers—and they

announced me as the winner. My design was featured on the annual art show invitation for all to see. It was a significant accomplishment. Kristi Kay was *someone*.

Back at the department store I watched in fascination as the visual merchandisers set up the displays and dressed the mannequins. As the storefronts came to life, my heart fluttered in a way it hadn't before. Watching and taking mental notes helped me prepare for the upcoming visual presentation project.

I browsed the aisles for ideas—animal prints were everywhere. A wild safari theme for the win! The display wasn't all about the outfit but also the accessories, signage, and props, then putting them all together. Ms. Pohl was impressed and noticed I had a visual eye that came naturally—not something every fashion student possessed. Why not consider a career as a window dresser? Visual merchandising positions were coveted in the early 1990s.

During my college years, life was happy and easy, and I felt especially empowered by using my God-given talents such as those related to fashion. Having character and strong morals was equally important. There were many other skills to develop before graduation—it was coming fast.

Fashion majors met at a swanky hotel and conference center for an all-day business and etiquette seminar. It would prepare us for the many required on-site workshops with top vendors throughout the city, giving us a behind-the-scenes look into the fashion industry. But first—a shopping spree!

The girls and I rummaged through racks of gently used name-brand clothes at a trendy consignment shop. We didn't have to spend a fortune to look good. The tailored slacks and cashmere sweater I was wearing looked impressionable as did the camel coat draped over my arm. Goodbye, college students—hello, sassy, classy fashionistas! We all took home bags of treasures and a new professional style, ready to tackle our internships.

For six weeks I worked at the small chain store at the strip mall with three other gals. We swayed to the music while tagging, steaming, and hanging up the latest apparel. But I also learned a multitude of managing skills. At its completion, a job as a visual merchandiser was a better fit, where my creative outlets could roam free. Managing a store—not so much.

My thoughts return to the here and now, stretched out by the fireplace with my college boxes. Everything *passion and fashion*—paintings, illustrations, and my cherished portfolio. In it was a captivating five-by-seven photograph. I was dressed to the nines and stood in front of a stage. It was just like yesterday.

It was the night of the fashion show, held at one of the city's historic venues, in a charming hall at the train station. Hundreds of glitter earth globes hung from the ceiling for the global togetherness theme, inspired by New York and American house band Deee-Lite's hit album *World Clique*. Its music was featured during the show.

Behind the scenes, $25,000 worth of apparel was on loan from the department store. Fashion students, models, and crew scurried to finish the final touches, including the light and sound checks. This was our moment! The countdown—five, four, three, two, one!

Microphone in hand, Ms. Pohl shouted, "It's a go!"

The music, bold and sassy, a little retro, and a wee bit funky. The models swaggered down the runway in the latest hip hoppy, larger-than-life vibe. Bold. Edgy. Vibrant. A sign of the times. With a shift of the music, models swayed easy–peasy to the monochromatic silhouettes in hues of gray and soft knits. At the end of the catwalk came the iconic turn and pose.

As the last song blared over the speakers, the girls and I strutted down the runway and raised our hands together for a final bow. The audience loved the hour-long show and applauded. It was like being on an episode of *Style of Elsa Klensch*. Little-girl dreams had come true, if only for a moment. A week later, each classmate walked across the stage and was presented with a degree in fashion merchandising.

God gave me a lifelong passion for fashion, and I still scribble in a sketchbook, enjoy shopping for just about anything, and ogle over the Louis Vuittons. You will also find me dancing to the music if the beat is right. Darlings, *groove is in my heart.*

CHAPTER 4

The Love of a Family

She speaks with wisdom, and faithful instruction is on her tongue. She watches over the affairs of her household. . . . Her children arise and call her blessed.
—Proverbs 31:26–28

"Love will hold us together."
—Matt Maher

Outside on the patio I enjoy breakfast in the warmth of the sun on a beautiful June morning. As I gaze at the blooming flowers, a gentle breeze blows through my hair and I remember holding a delicate bouquet and being excited about starting a family of my own.

Across a field of brome grass was a tiny white church. Its steeple could be seen for miles. Inside, the wedding of my dreams took place. Family and friends stood proudly while Dad walked me down the aisle. The white gown and beaded headpiece made me feel like a princess. At the altar I joined hands with Derek, my love of five years. Two became one in the eyes of God. After the ceremony, we danced cheek to cheek to our favorite song, and he promised to love me forever.

A honeymoon to the lake brought much-needed relaxation.

Fishing on the pontoon was just what we needed before returning to our jobs a week later.

We lived in the city for nearly five years, but were growing weary of the busyness, so we started looking for an acreage. After a year, small town called us back home.

The ranch-style house was picture-perfect inside and out, sitting on two acres on the edge of a village of about 342 residents. At the end of our first day at our new home, Derek and I retired to the backyard to relax. The neighbor lady welcomed us with freshly baked chocolate chip cookies, and while chatting, she inquired about children. Derek and I grinned. Not quite yet, but what a wonderful place to raise a family, and the house had plenty of room when the time came. We could almost hear the pitter-patter of little feet.

After three weeks of getting settled, I started a new job at a local nursing home, which was only an eight-mile drive. My coworkers welcomed me to the dietary department, and a gal with a brown bob and I worked side by side. She spoke with a soft accent, and I found out she had just moved from Indiana, was married, and had an eleven-year-old son. Conversation flowed easily, and we became close friends.

I usually arrived home at eight in the evening and waited for Derek. Both of us worked second shifts for years and were accustomed to the late nights—it was our normal and we cuddled in the oversized recliner together while watching TV. Before we knew it, August's heat turned into December's cold. It was going to be a month to remember.

The two of us huddled in the bathroom at first light one morning, and our eyes fell upon a positive home pregnancy test—we were going to be parents! We wasted no time making phone calls to our families and friends.

While coworkers gathered for lunch in the break room, they shared my excitement and gave me a special gift—a journal for expectant mothers. I jotted down in the journal an ongoing record of special moments throughout the pregnancy. Heartbeats, sonograms, cravings, and even baby's movements were noted.

Close friends who were also expecting shared popular books and magazines with fascinating pictures of a growing fetus week by week, which made it easy to track the baby's development. But carrying a baby was exhausting!

The California King bed was ideal for reading or napping, especially when Derek lay next to me with his hands over my growing belly. He whispered sweet messages that only a first-time father-to-be could give. Tender. Loving. And as the pregnancy progressed, he read books out loud to the baby. We were excited when the baby responded to our voices with gentle kicks. But even more amazing was that there was really a tiny human inside my womb—truly a miracle from God. In these moments we easily bonded.

Nine months passed by quickly. The August heat was unforgiving on my body, creating swollen hands, swollen feet, and a lingering backache. I longed for labor to start. At a routine checkup, it was discovered that the baby was active and healthy, but the amniotic fluid was dangerously low, so an induction was scheduled for a few days later. Derek and I rushed home to put the finishing touches on the nursery.

The mint-green walls would welcome a boy or a girl, as did the colorful cartoon border, matching pictures, and bed set. I relaxed in the antique rocking chair while Derek put the sheets, bumper pad, and quilt on the crib. When it was complete, he held my hands while whispering, "Hey, Momma"—and then we went to town, me waddling, for more items for newborns.

On the day of the induction, a nurse checked us into the hospital and placed us in a birthing suite. We giggled about how to put on my hospital gown. If even this was a problem, how on earth would we be able to take care of a newborn? The labor and delivery nurse told us what to expect as she administered Pitocin into the IV.

Powerful contractions became unbearable throughout the day. No video or book could have prepared us for childbirth. After seven hours, I begged for an epidural to relieve the pain. It would also give me a chance to rest. Derek had a chance to update the family and set up the camcorder.

Pushing for hours was hard work. Derek held my hand the entire time while nurses assisted the doctor, who instructed, "One more push."

It was a boy—and we named him Michael. His cry was healthy and he had a head full of dark hair just like his daddy's. As the doctor placed him onto my chest, tears rolled down Derek's cheeks—a son to carry on the family name. It was love at first sight.

Late in the evening Derek went home to sleep. I held Michael closely, all the while thanking God and praying for protection and guidance. There is no other joy like being a mother—it's a forever joy.

Derek returned in the morning with flowers and beanie babies. The grandparents flocked behind him, holding balloons and gift bags. Happiness flooded the tiny room.

When we returned home the next day, Derek and I realized that parenting was truly a twenty-four-hour job, and sleep was scarce, so we appreciated help from loved ones. Friends brought outfits, toys, and—certainly one of the best gifts for new parents—meals. Since we were of the Chrisitan faith, a baptism was planned. Despite my strong Methodist upbringing, Derek insisted our children be raised Catholic as he was.

The private ceremony was held after mass at the Catholic church. Michael wore a special white satin suit and baptismal ring that was worn for generations on my father's side. The priest blessed him with holy water and welcomed him into a new life with God.

Time flew by quickly! Michael was on the move with his one-handed "army crawl." He was fast too. His eyes were full of wonder as he explored the living room and played with toys—but, of course, found more amusement with the cardboard boxes. Soon he uttered his first words and spoke a jargon only a parent could understand. Thank goodness for cameras and camcorders to catch every moment.

By summer's end, loved ones gathered on the patio for Michael's first birthday party, where *we* opened his gifts and let *him* eat his cake. He demolished it and he was covered from head to toe in white frosting. After the party Derek and I put him in the tub, all the while gazing into his eyes and whispering lovingly, "Are you ready for another one?" He smiled from ear to ear. We were so content.

Cold November days have replaced June's blooms. I'm wrapped up in a Pendleton blanket, and the wind rocks my hammock as I stare at the sky. It's dark and depressed, like my mood. I am remembering the day part of me died.

Two pink lines appeared on the pregnancy test! We were overjoyed to be expecting again, but a day or so later, cramping began in my lower abdomen. A doctor examined me in the emergency room. Blood work confirmed an early pregnancy, but there was no reason to worry or stay in the hospital, so Derek and I returned home.

Four weeks later at a routine obstetric appointment at the medical clinic, the doctor used a Doppler device on my belly, but there were no *swish-swish* sounds, so a sonogram was ordered. Maybe a heartbeat could be found on it. But what we saw on the screen was horrifying—a lifeless image. Our baby was dead. We held each other and cried in disbelief. This couldn't be happening to us.

Moments later the physician confirmed our worst nightmare, and the nurse sent us home with instructions. My body didn't miscarry naturally over the coming days as it should have. A repeat sonogram was necessary and we saw the lifeless image *again*. It was torture. But worse yet, the doctor ordered dilation and curettage. The procedure itself sounded excruciating and cruel.

After surgery I woke up in a private room alone, wrapped up in a fluffy pink robe that Derek had dropped off, and wept for hours. My heart and spirit were crushed, traumatized by the most painful, dead emotion that I had ever experienced. I questioned the Lord over and over, *Why did you take my baby? Why do you make me suffer?*

Back at home I lay on the couch for days, suffocating from depression. No one could help me, certainly not Derek or Michael. I pushed them away.

Our baby's death left me in pieces because I didn't get to hold her and there was no funeral to say goodbye. Besides, it was impossible to forget since there were reminders all around me. Newborns in strollers. Pregnant women at every store. Even three close friends who hid their growing bellies from me. I became angry at everyone, including God, and began calling out to Him, *Why did you abandon me when I needed you the most? Why won't you take my pain away?* It seemed that God had turned a deaf ear to me, so I began journaling my thoughts to cope with the loss. An excerpt:

> We named our baby Jordan because I needed closure. I feel very empty and dead on the inside and feel as if part of me died too. I will always feel this way. People make me feel worse when they unknowingly ask how far along I am and when others say, "You were only six weeks along—it wasn't really a baby anyway." I correct them. No—six weeks, five days. Hands, feet, fingers, and toes. This was *my* child and she will be waiting for me in heaven someday.

The thought lingered and couldn't get it out of my head. Was Jordan really in heaven? Surely our friends in the pastoral care office at the Catholic hospital could provide answers and comfort. They were just a phone call away. A meeting was planned.

Peace enveloped the tiny chapel, and a small stained-glass window brought comfort. We gathered on the wooden pews to chat. I showed them the picture of Jordan, now in a silver angel frame.

The nuns were very reassuring, telling me to rejoice—Jordan *was* in heaven! We prayed hand in hand and lit a candle at the altar in her memory. A tremendous burden was lifted. Knowing she was with God brought relief. Someday I'll meet her in heaven.

After the visit, Chaplain Anne had a special request—an invitation for Derek and me to be guest speakers at an upcoming infant loss memorial service. What a privilege it would be to share our story with other grieving parents! It felt as if God was reaching out to us. How could we say no?

"Under His Wings" was held at a charming brick church near the hospital. Soft piano music played throughout the sanctuary, which was filled with families, nuns, and my chaplain friend, who offered the opening prayer.

Derek held Michael while I spoke softly about our loss and recited the poem "What Makes a Mother." The words brought everyone to tears, including me. Then we returned to our seats.

Another couple came forward, and the husband gave his perspective. Derek was bawling, and it was then that I realized he was grieving too. Up until that moment I hadn't even given it a thought. Not only mothers lose babies. Acknowledging his pain as a father was important and necessary.

The service also included a short message about faith and hope and concluded with a beautiful solo about angels. We could all feel each other's pain, but also God's Spirit was moving. At this moment true healing began. Perhaps in the midst of all this, God had a purpose for Jordan's passing—whether it was to help others navigate through the grieving process or at least to let other parents know that they weren't alone. God gave me the gift of speech—and for that I was grateful.

The crowd gathered in the fellowship hall for refreshments while the nuns handed out felt angel wings and packets of flower seeds to the parents to plant in memory of their babies. What a wonderful way to honor them!

As we said our goodbyes, Sister Caroline placed a silver chain around my neck with a pendant of Saint Gerard, patron to expectant mothers, and a booklet of novena prayers to recite daily. Together they were believed to offer protection for conception, the duration of pregnancy, and delivery. The gift was cherished immensely, and I never once removed the necklace from that day forward.

Weeks later Chaplain Anne called to thank us again for speaking at the memorial service and also invited Derek and me to speak for an upcoming obstetric in-service. Sharing our story was healing in itself, so we joined two other couples who had lost their babies as well. Together we shared personal perspectives of miscarriage, stillbirth, and sudden infant death syndrome—and spoke candidly with the nurses. It was important for them to understand the emotional and physical details in different stages of loss.

After the in-service, each couple was given an angel teddy bear and a certificate in honor of our babies, which Derek and I framed and placed on the wall at home. Jordan would always be a part of our family. Her life *and* death were finally celebrated, which brought remarkable peace.

Derek reminded me to cope in a positive way. Michael was alive and needed our full attention and love. We never told him about the baby but knew he sensed our sadness. It was important for us to remember that *he* was full of life.

The California King bed was a place to bond. Derek and I were grateful for the simple moments that brought healing through the grieving process. Our son brought us back to life with his charismatic smile and laughter. Each day got easier.

Six months passed by, and we were shocked by the news of another pregnancy so soon. Naturally, we tiptoed cautiously through the first trimester and didn't tell a soul. The doctor suggested cutting back my hours at work and resting more. Each day I faithfully recited the novena prayers and trusted that God was helping protect our unborn child.

Now two years old, Michael named my growing belly "My Baby." He kissed it, cradled it, and even put little headphones around it and played music. Also at night we used the newest home doppler system to hear the baby's movement and heartbeat—the *swish-swish* sounds of life. Explaining the role of big brother to Michael was amusing to say the least.

Michael said goodbye to the nursery and helped his daddy redecorate the guest bedroom. Laughter filled the room as they painted the walls and each other a pretty shade of blue, then added colorful curtains, a toddler bed, and toybox. Next door in the bathroom was a pint-sized potty. Our big boy didn't need diapers anymore, but "My Baby" would. We knew life was going to become very busy, so we relished our rests on the California King bed.

Days later, contractions started prematurely. At the hospital the doctor ordered a battery of tests. An overnight stay was warranted. IV medications stopped labor altogether. Back at home, it was bed rest for the duration of the pregnancy.

Dad and Mae joined us for a late Thanksgiving lunch. Two hours after eating sweet potatoes, my labor began again—we weren't having a Christmas baby after all! Thank goodness, they were able to step in and watch over Michael while Derek and I were at the hospital. It certainly was perfect timing, part of God's plan for sure.

We walked the halls for hours and returned to our room for rest. At the crack of dawn the doctor broke my water and brutal contractions began, causing horrific pain. Something was wrong. Derek ran to get a nurse.

To her surprise, my cervix was fully dilated. She quickly wheeled me into the delivery room and gave strict orders *not* to push. What was all the commotion about? Nurses scattered all around until the doctor arrived. I gave birth almost effortlessly. The absence of a newborn cry was frightening. Chaos filled the room. Maybe we had had another dead baby.

Derek held my hand and calmly explained our *son* was blue and not breathing because the umbilical cord was wrapped around his neck. Lukus needed oxygen for a while and he would be closely monitored. In that moment I understood why labor had happened so fast and grasped the Saint Gerard pendant and prayed. God protected our baby.

A few hours later, Lukus was finally in my arms. He was handsome, and his tiny face and dark hair resembled that of his big brother. They were almost identical at birth.

Later, Derek arrived and carried Michael over to the bed and placed him by my side. He showed off his big brother T-shirt and gently kissed Lukus. "My Baby, My Baby," he chanted, just as proud as ever. And just like that, our family of four was complete.

Dad and Mae stayed with us for an entire week. They helped with the nursery, prepared meals, and tended to the laundry. We couldn't have done it without them. When they went back to Kansas, Derek's parents took over and showered Lukus with gifts and attention. In the evening we shared a meal and discussed the baptism.

A blizzard the night before left drifts of snow everywhere, so the gathering at the church was small. Lukus wore the birthing suit and Grandpa's ring, tied to his finger with a tiny blue ribbon. As Father blessed Lukus with holy water, the sun shone through the windows. We felt God's love and protection, not knowing the struggles that lay ahead.

Lukus vomited after every nursing and failed to gain weight, even when we switched him to formula. All of his lymph nodes were swollen, which was concerning—the doctor even hinted at Hodgkins disease. We were all gravely concerned about his brain development from malnourishment and insisted on a thorough analysis.

The female physician's assistant was mild-mannered and

empathetic. Right away she recognized specific symptoms that mirrored that of her own son. It was clear to her that Lukus was most likely having digestive issues related to an allergy. She sent us to a pediatric gastroenterologist at the medical center.

Lukus was diagnosed with MSPI (milk soy protein intolerance). Simply put, it's an allergic reaction to all milk and soy and any other byproducts, and he was placed on a strict diet of tube-feeding formula via bottle for a minimum of eighteen months. He could not consume any other food—no exceptions. We were given samples to take home.

The special formula was available online only—and it was expensive, almost six dollars per bottle. As the months passed by, our credit card was maxed out. What parent is prepared for a major medical event? Maybe God was using our struggle to help others again.

Derek and I had to educate ourselves, our families, and the daycare provider since MSPI wasn't mainstream. We didn't want Lukus to start the long process over again by accidental ingestion of food. Slowly he began to gain weight.

Finally, after eighteen months on a liquid diet and having skipped baby food altogether, Lukus started the slow process of learning how to swallow solid food with the assistance of a speech and language pathologist. It was interesting watching him try new tastes and textures.

By Lukus's second birthday, he was a normal toddler, showing no signs of impairment whatsoever. In fact, he was lively, intelligent, and met every milestone. Sighs of relief. There were only happy days ahead.

June has returned, and I'm back on the patio, lounging in the sun. Kids are laughing and frolicking on the jungle gym next door. Seeing them makes me smile—and it seems like yesterday when my boys were playing on the Slip 'N Slide and drinking from the hose on a hot summer day.

The backyard was scattered with a sandbox, Tonka trucks, other toys, and a tiny swimming pool. In the pool was Lukus, holding a bucket and a ball. Behind him was his big brother with a Super Soaker and a priceless grin. When playtime ended, a trail of muddy footprints could be found throughout the house. But the messes always made me smile—well, most of the time.

The boys were my heart's delight, even when they dragged me out of bed on a Saturday morning. In the living room were cartoons and chaos—Matchbox cars, Legos, and colorful sugar-coated rings everywhere. "Mommy, look—we got our *own* cereal!" said Lukus—but it looked like more of a food fight and brotherly love. Never a dull moment, and I wouldn't have it any other way because there was so much more fun to be had.

Brothers snuggled on the blanket to watch cartoons. When *Bob the Builder* came on, the little fix-its danced to the theme song in their bib overalls, plastic tool sets in hand. They couldn't wait to help their daddy when he returned home for the day.

They worked together to replace the front door. A tap here, a tap there, and then Michael's hammer went wild. A broken window, a crack in the door, then a roll of the tongue! Then a new jacuzzi tub was installed by the magnificent three. Lukus was the first to jump in. There were bubbles up to the ceiling. What parent could be mad?

In the kitchen a pot of chili and freshly baked cinnamon rolls marked the first day of hunting season. The boys pranced around in a hodge-podge of oversized camouflage and neon orange and ran outside when Derek returned and his headlights shone in the driveway. "Look at that—a ten point buck! Can we help clean it?" shouted Michael. The trio could be found in the kitchen making jerky in the days to come. Derek used every moment to teach the boys.

Cold, snowy days were the best for hanging out in the kitchen, whether it was sipping cocoa or baking cookies. In the late afternoon a wonderful smell came from the oven. Meatloaf was always a hit. We had just enough time to pull out the old whirley pop and make Grandma's 3-2-1 candied popcorn, a favorite snack.

As a family we nestled together in the living room for a double feature every Friday night. But it was more like a movie theater since Derek had installed a new TV set and state-of-the-art surround sound. The simplest moments were the best—and plenty of time to enjoy them over the winter months.

Snowfall turned into rain and we watched the tulips rise out of the soil. It was finally spring. Brothers could always be found splashing around in the puddles—but their footprints were a bit bigger now.

The backyard was a place of joy, laughter, and innocence. The boys could always be found jumping on the trampoline. Imagine my amusement when the new puppy was bouncing up and down with them! "Look, Mommy!" said Lukus. "Odie's up here with us!" All I could do was laugh—and join them.

Summer wasn't all play as there was much work to do as a family in the garden. Behind the shed was freshly tilled soil. The boys helped plant tiny seeds, covered them, and marked each row with a stake. Then Derek placed a custom-built six-foot-high sprinkler in the middle. Every day the boys inspected every inch of the garden for new seedlings emerging out of the soil—it was their very own science experiment!

Ten feet away was a stunning strawberry patch. The birds kept pecking at the ripe fruit, so we needed a plan. The brothers sat on the patio and painted small rocks bright red and placed them around the perimeter. Boy, did it work! There were plenty of berries for homemade pies and shortcakes throughout the summer.

The boys came running one day when they heard the John Deere—that meant a ride with Mommy. Little hands fit over mine as they steered and cheered. For hours they took turns making passes over the lawn. The baggers were unloaded and the grass clippings were used to mulch the garden. We finished just in time. The sky darkened and the temperature dropped—a storm was moving in fast. The wind shifted, a bang of thunder, and a strike of lightning. The town sirens blared, so the boys and I took cover in the basement. When it hailed, we sneaked back outside. The ground was covered with tiny white pebbles. They scooped them up and watched them melt in their hands. It was a wonderful sight to see.

In an instant, sunlight peeked through the clouds, and a spectrum of rainbow colors appeared in all their majestic beauty—which brought a peaceful feeling. I realized in this moment that I would always be a girly-girl mom of two messy little boys, and that was the way God intended it. Any residual longing for a girl disappeared just as the rainbow did.

The days became shorter and cooler, and then it was harvest time. Michael hooked up a wagon to Great-Grandpa's red pedal tractor and drove it to the south edge of the garden where potatoes were dug. Lukus and I filled baskets with a palette of colorful vegetables and ate peas right out of the pod. Tomatoes and jalapeños were ripe for the picking so I grabbed a handful and headed indoors to make fresh salsa and a feast.

Tiki torches lit up the backyard. Derek fired up the grill and showed his sons how it was done. Burgers and brats could be smelled from the kitchen, but also the fresh strawberry- rhubarb pies that were baking in the oven.

Soon the best of friends arrived. We enjoyed a meal and small talk at the picnic table. After supper, the boys and their pint-sized friends ran around in the darkness, chasing lightning bugs and placing them in mason jars. The magical glow was mesmerizing. Who doesn't remember doing that as a child?

The end of summer brought a trip to the county fair, where we tiptoed through the animal barn. Engines revved while watching the figure-eight races and demo derby in the grandstand. And at dusk, a trip down the midway—carnival rides for hours and a generous supply of cotton candy. The best of times had by all.

Summer wouldn't be complete without a family photograph taken at the park. The photographer led us for a short walk along the trails with the perfect place in mind. We sat in the grass and leaned up against a tall oak tree, all huddled together. The shrubs, creek, and bridge behind us made the perfect backdrop. Laughter brought smiles, and with the flash of the camera the love of a family was caught forever. Nothing would ever tear us apart.

CHAPTER 5

The Diagnosis

*Truly my soul finds rest in God; my salvation comes
from him. Truly he is my rock and my salvation;
he is my fortress, I will never be shaken.*
—Psalm 62:1–2

"I'm tired. I'm worn. My heart is heavy."
—Tenth Avenue North

The basement is the only place of respite. The shag carpet tickles my bare feet while walking to the crushed velvet swivel chair in the corner. Grandmother's Afghan is heavy and the weight of it is calming as is swinging my legs back and forth. The demands of a full-time employee, wife, and mother are taking their toll. Instinct tells me something is about to shift.

No one likes getting called in on his or her day off. I grudgingly rolled out of bed, quickly showered, and drove to work. My mind was full of chaos, but so was the short-staffed kitchen. A coworker and I argued. The boss called me into her office demanding an explanation. Not knowing what was wrong with me, I ran to the locker room, grabbed my purse, and drove to the nearby medical clinic, where I frantically called my stepmother.

Mae knew by the sound of my voice that something was wrong. "Kristi, I'm concerned. Do you want to harm yourself?" My silence spoke the truth. Her voice was reassuring. She cared a great deal about my well-being.

A doctor saw me immediately, but he couldn't help and sent me to the mental health clinic downtown. I waited alone in a room for over thirty minutes, frightened and anxious. After a brief visit, the counselor called Derek at work. He had to drive me to the hospital in the city for a psychiatric examination. We didn't understand what was happening. Neither of us said a single word during the hour-long drive.

Triage was noisy and cluttered with patients. After an hour's wait, I was admitted and given a pill to help the anxiety. Not seeing my children made the situation worse. But then Dad and Mae arrived and sat close to the bed. Derek left for home, which was okay because it gave us time to talk privately. There was concern in Dad's eyes. Truth be told, I had never been as anxious since high school. They stayed until visiting hours were over, leaving me all alone again in a strange place.

The hospital cubicle was chilly. I curled up in a ball on the gurney with a coarse white blanket. It was difficult to get comfortable. My mind and body raced all night, tossing and turning to the clock. Tick, tock, tick, tock.

In the morning a nurse took me to the fourth-floor psychiatric department and into a locked unit, the adult affective disorders (AAD) unit. A private room was at the end of the hall, consisting of a bed, pillow, and nightstand. I was monitored every half hour since the doctor placed me on mandatory suicide watch. It was a lonely and frightening place to be. And it wasn't until the next day that the psychiatrist paid a visit. He spoke only medical terminology that I didn't understand as I sulked on the bed, feeling worthless. The awkward and timid Kristi Kay had reemerged.

The Diagnosis

Mom visited the next day and brought a sack full of clothes. A lavender sweatsuit from Kmart was not my style. I rolled my eyes at Mom-and we cracked a half-smile. But moments of silence followed and she noted a definite shift in my mood. There was an absence of emotion, and darkness had come about me. When she left, I was alone again and longed for my children.

Shortly thereafter, the psychiatrist added privileges, which allowed me to shower and then attend small-group therapy, located in the conference room, where a certified counselor led the conversation among a handful of teens and a few middle-aged adults. Talk was candid as patients shared their stories of what brought them into the AAD unit, which included their frightening suicide attempts, and I quickly learned the harsh truth about mental health disorders—but I didn't say anything since *I* wasn't like *them*. My meltdown was a product of exhaustion and working too many hours alongside raising young boys. Surely I would bounce back by the end of the week and just needed rest. After the sixth day, Derek and the boys picked me up.

Michael and Lukus were puzzled by my absence at home and had many questions during the drive home. Derek thought "tired" was the best answer.

While walking into the house, I stopped dead in my tracks—everything was *un*done and it looked like a tornado had blown through it. Laundry overflowed from the hamper, dirty dishes were piled up, and evidence of two busy toddlers were obvious in every nook and cranny. I was livid at Derek—it would take weeks to catch up on housework. Didn't he care about *my* feelings and fragility?

I had another psychological exam a week later. The psychiatrist told me the formal diagnosis–Bipolar Disorder. The two words seemed like a death sentence with a lifetime prescription for lithium. But wasn't that for crazy people? I started taking the medication immediately, and the side efforts were horrible. My body needed time to adjust. A calm place came to mind.

Dad and Mae's acreage was a perfect getaway. Walking in the country, taking a dip in the hot tub and napping helped me relax. By Saturday, I felt well enough to go to town and browse a few thrift shops with Dad. It was no coincidence when I stumbled across a Bible on a shelf much like that of my childhood Bible. God was reminding me He was with me—or rather carrying me once again. I took it with me to church the next morning.

Dad introduced me to the pastor and a few members before we took our seats. The sanctuary was comforting. Mae played the piano beautifully. We sang familiar hymns, and then the bell choir played. The sound of them was magnificent and woke up my spirit, because it was a reminder of happy times when I was closer to God. But it quickly faded and my heart turned melancholy because the "trip" would soon be over. Dad reminded me to have faith and that everything would be fine, and to live day by day. Oh, how he loved his daughter, and I loved him right back. I returned home with a fair frame of mind.

Lithium therapy was intolerable. Side effects included pounding headaches and a hand tremor that worsened over the weeks. Agitation and insomnia followed. Working full time and caring for my family exacerbated it, and it didn't take much to anger me.

I waited for Derek in the dark one day. When he walked through the front door after work, tempers flared. Why couldn't he help around the house? Why couldn't he help with the kids? Why couldn't he spend time with me? Kristi Kay felt abandoned again. Without hesitation, I swallowed a handful of sleeping pills and threw the empty bottle at him, "Now you don't have to worry about me—ever!" I screamed.

The Diagnosis

The sirens screamed. Paramedics rushed me to the emergency room. Charcoal was administered from a tube and forced down my throat, and I slowly awoke while gagging on it and vomited all over the nurse. She gave me a dirty look and sarcastically said, "I'll bet you never do that again." Then the doctor chimed in too. "You *really* don't want to die, do you?"

Their condescending tone was degrading. Later, a smug bald man visited. He was the on-call therapist and wasn't happy about the late-night visit. "All you want is attention," he said. He didn't take my actions seriously. "It wasn't my first time." I wanted to give him a piece of my mind, but couldn't. Words danced around in my head: *Seriously, dude. Thanks for caring. I just OD'ed and all you can do is talk to me like I'm stupid? Do you not understand how worthless you are making me feel right now? You do not know the pain I am in. Next time I'll swallow the whole bottle of pills and sit in my garage until the job is done. How would you like that? Don't you dare judge me or even pretend to know what I am feeling. You have no clue what I'm going through!*

We retired home and Derek put me in bed. But then he leaned in close and told me how stupid I was, because Michael had awoken during the commotion and watched the first responders. The guilt and shame were overwhelming. Derek was right. What kind of mother would do that? The "Why bother?" syndrome set in, and the suicidal ideation worsened. Another inpatient visit was necessary, so we drove to another facility.

This hospital was different. A nurse gave us the grand tour down the corridor with cheerful yellow walls leading to the psychiatric unit. The smell of eucalyptus was calming, and there was a spacious commons area with a TV, lounge, and micro-library. It certainly didn't look like a mental institution– and neither did the private room. Michael and Lukus pulled out handmade pictures for me to keep during the stay, and they put them on the magnetic board.

Derek told them mommy needed to rest. They seemed more at ease knowing the where and the why. Staying positive was important—we were all going to be okay.

Patients gathered in the commons. They were friendly, mostly female, and I was encouraged by their stories of bipolar disorder and anxiety—and also spoke to a young man with schizophrenia. Mental illness was more common than I had thought—we were all ordinary people! I felt a sense of belonging because I wasn't alone anymore.

Later a young female psychiatrist with curly, brown hair stopped by for an evaluation. I shared my feelings and concerns with her without judgment. She explained there were many treatment options for bipolar disorder. In time, my body would adjust to the medications, and eventually the cycling would slow down in intensity and duration. In the meantime, adapting and learning positive coping skills were the new normal.

The art therapy room had colorful murals on the walls. It was a cozy space full of supplies, including easels, canvases, journals, and tubs of paint in every color. And in the corner were pottery and a kiln!

An "aha" moment! Surely the artistic Kristi Kay was still inside. Every day we patients gathered together to create just about anything while talking about our feelings and diagnoses, and we exchanged coping skills. The best way to learn about it was firsthand. It was then I realized how individualized bipolar was. I had to find the right meds and therapy for *me*, whatever it looked like. Maybe, just maybe, it wasn't the end of the world.

A sense of hope returned, especially when the boys came running into the unit when I was released to go home. It was good to see Derek too, and they had a surprise—we dined at a fine steakhouse and even splurged on dessert. By the time we arrived home, it was bedtime. Watching the boys wiggle into their zip-up footie pajamas brought delight as did tucking them in and giving them butterfly kisses. It was good to be home. Finally—some alone time with Derek.

As I lay next to him in bed, he studied me, as if I were different and damaged beyond repair. Or maybe the hospital had fixed me and Kristi would return. In my mind were two parallels just like the bipolar disorder that had affected the entire family. Our lives had been turned completely upside down without any warning. We had no idea what the future held. There were so many uncertainties. Sometimes it was easier to say nothing at all, so I simply shut off the light.

In the morning I met with a licensed mental health therapist named Charlene. She was thin, about fifty, and wore a frilly dress. Charlene explained cognitive behavior therapy. The goal was for me to understand the diagnosis, process emotions, and implement positive coping skills. But also, learning how to accept my limitations in daily life was key. The session went quickly and Charlene escorted me to the next room.

The psychiatrist was a tall, dark-skinned man who spoke with an accent. He prescribed all the medications and monitored shifts in mood. They didn't level out, so he added more, including a high dose of an antipsychotic, which caused a plethora of side effects, including brain fog, tiredness, and blood sugar fluctuation. The depression was relentless. Nothing or no one could help me, so I quit therapy altogether. It didn't seem to me that God cared either. Why not just disappear?

A stranger looked back at me in the vanity mirror. *Who is this pudgy woman with black eyes and scraggly hair?* The bathroom scale isn't friendly either, since I've gained a whopping sixty pounds in just a year's time. The bipolar meds are to blame and they make me forage through the cupboards at night for Pop-Tarts, cookies—anything sweet. I looked at my body in disgust. I was fat again and hated it. The emotional pain was overwhelming and had to be dealt with.

I rummaged through Derek's toolbox and found a straight razor blade, locked myself in the bedroom, and made cuts on my legs. As the blood trickled, relief came—the pain was gone for just a moment. Sometimes the cuts were deep when inflicted by broken glass and left permanent scars. Panic set in. There had to be another way to find relief, so I begged my doctor for more pills. It was so easy to get them.

A collection of benzodiazepines and hypnotics were well hidden in a secret stash in the bedroom. After the boys fell asleep at night, I took them—white ones, pink ones, maybe a blue one too. Moments later the pain faded away.

Dad and Mae often called shortly after nine in the evening. My words were always slurred. They could see through the "I'm just tired" facade. Derek had his suspicions too. One night he found me passed out on the couch when he returned home from work and carried me to bed. But at other times I barely had a pulse, so the rescue unit would rush me to the hospital. After the seventh trip, the ER doc asked what I had taken and how many. Derek was furious and demanded a toxicology report. The secret was out. In the car he screamed.

"The ambulance rides are costing us a fortune! Figure it out and quit embarrassing the family! Everyone knows you're the town crazy, Kristi. Can't they fix you?"

I *hated* those words. Didn't he know how embarrassed and shameful *I* felt? How could my own husband be so callous about my mental health? The Kristi Kay he had married was fading away, and I knew it to be true. There was no choice but to return to therapy.

Dr. Varra was a clinical psychologist who specialized in the diagnosis and treatment of mental illness. He was short, Hispanic, and had a kind bedside manner. He was noticeably intelligent, even though he was just out of college. He spoke gently and proved to be trustworthy.

I shared my innermost feelings and purged every secret, including the past suicide attempts, the eating disorder, the addiction, and the self-mutilation. I even brought the blades to him in a jar. That caught him off guard, but he could see the desperation. Dr. Varra was certain he could help me understand the diagnosis, which was half the battle.

After weeks of therapy, he reaffirmed the diagnosis of bipolar disorder type 2, mixed. But there was more. The symptoms overlapped. Borderline personality disorder coexisted, which explained the self-esteem and abandonment issues and frequent mood swings. As therapy continued over a period of months, I began sharing even more.

Nightmares plagued my sleep and flashbacks during the day, blurred images that caused anxiety, fear, and hypervigilance—all symptoms of PTSD (post-traumatic stress disorder). Dr. Varra explained that the brain was complex and had the ability to bury trauma. Bits and pieces came together. They stemmed from college, but the memories were too painful to talk about.

Three mental disorders were intertwined together, which made treatment more difficult. I was a mental mess. Dr. Varra gave crucial advice: "Kristi, you have a lifetime chronic illness for which there is no cure. You are still in the early stages of treatment. There is a very delicate balance you have to learn. Your health is very important, and you will need medications and therapy throughout your life. Many patients of mine cannot work outside the home, and that is nothing to be ashamed of. Please, do not work anymore, given your diagnosis and fragile state of mind. We can check into resources if you need them. But you must make your mental health your priority. The first step is getting you stable. Go home and talk to your husband. We can set up a time to meet if he has any questions."

A moment of silence. That was a lot to take in, but the words *stable* and *balance* brought comfort. The overall lifetime goal was to be in the middle—neither too up nor too down. Some patients call it the "flatline."

Derek and I had a heart-to-heart conversation over the weekend. Although it would be tough financially, we both agreed to take Dr. Varra's advice. It was hard leaving my work at the nursing home after seven years, but there was no other choice. It was an abrupt shift suddenly becoming a stay-at-home mom.

I bore all the responsibility of taking care of the home and the boys while Derek worked the three-to-eleven shift. The first week was overwhelming—the boys were so lively!

Who said being a stay-at-home mom was easy? What mom doesn't spend all her time cooking, tending to laundry, and cleaning up messes? The chaos was never-ending. The boys chased each other around the table with Nerf guns, and I got caught in the crossfire. Play-Doh was smashed into the carpet, and red Kool-Aid dripped off the counter onto the carpet, leaving a permanent stain. And no, that was not a grilled cheese sandwich in the VCR—true! Their shenanigans left me worn out and begging for a nap on the California King bed.

Quiet time didn't last long since Michael was a wiggle worm and kept tugging at my shirt. "Can we get up now? You promised we'd watch TV. Now! Let's go!"

So much for rest. Half asleep, we took our blankets to the living room and made camp on the floor. I was failing my children, and they could feel it too. Lukus touched my face and wiped my tears. "Mommy, why are you sad?"

His big, blue eyes were full of sensitivity. How had this toddler picked up on my sorrow? The three of us hugged tightly, and I realized what a gift from God they were. That was reason enough to keep going.

Several months passed by, and a new routine was well established. After lunch, Derek left for work early so he could pick up extra hours. The boys and I stayed at home most days because my anxiety was too overwhelming, especially when driving. But on Fridays we made one trip to town in the white sedan.

The Diagnosis

Our first stop was at a small thrift store where everything was a dollar, even clothes and shoes. We scavenged every rack for some new outfits while Michael and Lukus found their own treasures, including their pick of free books and toys.

We loaded into the car and drove off to the grocery store. They looked forward to riding in the cart, but I hated shopping since there was little money budgeted for food. Canned ravioli, frozen pizza, and cheap mac and cheese dotted the empty cart. And at the checkout I grudgingly wrote a check and hoped it cleared at the bank on Monday.

Back at home, the desk was covered in bills. We faced tens of thousands of dollars in debt since the insurance company paid very little on the hospital bills, therapy, and medications. The credit cards were maxed out and the bank had shut us off. No more loans, so hardship letters were written to every creditor. There was no end in sight. It was a disgusting feeling when I looked through the cushions for change to pay *something* on the shut-off notice, which added to my feelings of worthlessness.

Derek and I argued all the time about money. He blamed me for the financial ruin—but I never asked to be sick or have a mental illness and sincerely felt bad since he worked every weekend and used his bonus money to buy food. That made him resentful, and he drifted away into his own world of make-believe on his computer.

I lay outside one day in my favorite sweater, huddling under a heavy blanket. Only it knows my despair and secrets. My only relief is in a heavy metal song playing in the background. Fade. Drift. Lost. End. Free. I understand the lyrics and they understand me. I'm safe for the moment.

The changing of the seasons brought a little hope with the sun and warmer temperatures. I looked forward to time in the backyard with the boys, especially the garden and the heavy work it provided. Besides, I couldn't wait for my mania to set in, and when it did, I was full of energy and loved every minute. My mantra was "Two thousand tabs open all at the same time and no need for sleep." I was elated and could do *anything*. Go, go, go, get it done, get it done, get it done! The boys were happy, too—time with the fun mommy.

Under the moonlight the boys and I were plucking every piece of grass in the garden. Lukus was holding the flashlight and giggled because the new game was fun. We worked diligently for hours listening to the crickets chirping and other nighttime sounds. The fresh air was calming, and I yearned to feel this good all the time, not just in the moment. Mania was the polar opposite of depression.

The burst of energy lasted for days. There was an incessant need to keep my mind and hands busy. The house was cleaned from top to bottom, and we caught up on a couple years' worth of dust. Then a grand idea—why not paint and texturize the bathroom and hallway? It would take only a few hours. Splish, splash, and a crinkle of saran wrap on the wall. Michael and Lukus laughed, but Derek wasn't impressed with my bipolar artwork.

The kitchen smelled of a hot griddle and fresh pancakes everywhere—on the table, the counters, and even the floor. It seemed like hundreds! When the batter ran empty, we made a trip to the store and returned home to make scores more. The boys giggled, particularly when Derek stepped into the kitchen later.

Lukus held the flipper in the air. "Daddy, we're helping Mommy make *pan*cakes!" (and said it just like that).

The four of us giggled since we recognized mania for what it was in the moment: the wife and mom who was lighthearted and full of life. Everyone pitched in to clean up. Derek's smile turned into a frown because he knew the mania was at its peak and the dreaded crash was inevitable. Soon I would fall back into the pit.

Indeed, in the blink of an eye mental exhaustion set in. Loud and repetitive noises caused agitation. I screamed at the boys, even as they played innocently. Depression followed. The master bedroom was the only place to get relief. With the heavy drapes pulled shut, it was dark and quiet. Under the covers I begged God for just a moment of sleep. Just then the brothers burst through the doors. "Go away! Get out! I'm tired! Leave me alone!" I screamed and cursed until they cried and they ran to their father. What kind of mother was I, to use obscenities with my own children? This was the ugly side of bipolar disorder. It would only get worse.

Incomprehensible weariness settled over me because my brain wouldn't shut off. Sleep was impossible, especially since the weekend was over and Derek returned to work, which left me to tend to Michael and Lukus by myself.

All I could do was stare at them with blank eyes. Push, pull, yank, tug. "I want this, I want that," they said over and over. Suddenly they were the enemy, and I resented them. I felt shameful and guilty and drifted farther away. The boys could feel it too. Like the rest of the world, they hated me.

At my next appointment with Dr. Varra I was brutally honest about the darkness and suicidal ideation. I had nothing left to give the boys or my husband, my family, or the world. Dr. Varra required me to sign a suicide contract. That meant making a promise to call the office before acting. Rules had to be followed. If they were broken, he would hospitalize me again. Maybe it was better to stay quiet.

While sitting in my car I glanced into the rearview mirror and noticed those empty, dark eyes and a blank stare again. It was frightening, but I was simply worn out with everyday life and filled with self-hate. Little Girl Lost spoke the cold, hard truth.

"Lifetime illness, girl. You're broken and you're *never* coming back." The drive home was lonely and long. Maybe a semi would run into me so I didn't have to do it.

As the depression progressed, thoughts of death and dying creeped into my mind, and I asked myself numerous times *Do I really want to be dead? Maybe I just don't want to be alive.* There is a difference, you know.

Late at night I searched the Internet for ways to die and even printed off the information and bragged about it to Dr. Varra two days later. He was shocked by my audacity and insisted on hospitalization, but I balked, claiming that there was no plan in place. Deep down my thoughts were terrifying, and on the inside I was screaming for help. Would anyone listen? Would anyone understand? No! Not my husband, not my parents, not my friends. The doctor? Would he understand my most private thoughts? I didn't know, and it felt as if all I could do was hide the pain. Looking through the world with bipolar eyes made me feel ugly in every way.

While in town one afternoon I stopped at the library to find a couple books on heaven and hell, since I believed in both. After reading them, the latter got my attention since it was about one man's journey to hell. It was chilling! The demons, the beasts, the unfathomable pain and suffering described were confusing—especially regarding the fate of my own soul.

Desperate for answers, I stopped by the Catholic church and visited with the very priest who had baptized the boys. To him I was a stranger since we rarely attended mass. I explained the diagnosis and my feelings and asked him point blank, "Will I go to hell?" His answer was abrupt and insensitive. "You will go to hell if you commit suicide." I disagreed.

I explained further how hard living with bipolar disorder was and how bad the depressive episodes were. Father would never understand, and at this moment all hope was lost. I left the rectory feeling judged, rejected, and very alone.

As I walked through the front door, Derek and the boys were cuddling on the couch together and didn't seem to notice me at all. I didn't belong anywhere anymore.

The next day Derek took the boys to his parents' home since I refused to get out of bed. The thought of one more day was too much. The many diagnoses defeated me in every way—and something lured me to the basement, where I sat on the concrete floor and stared up at the black metal gun cabinet above me.

Satan had my Achilles heel and I heard an eerie cackle in the back of my mind. *You don't want to be here anymore. Just do it. All your pain will be gone. Just do it.*

Darkness surrounded me. Tears flowed from my eyes, my heart raced, and numbness took over my mind, body, and soul. I surrendered in the moment and whispered faintly, "Dear God, forgive me for what I'm about to do. I can't take it anymore."

CHAPTER 6

Bipolar Meets God

Be strong and courageous. Do not be afraid or terrified because of them, for the Lord your God goes with you; he will never leave you nor forsake you.
—Deuteronomy 31:6

"Lift up your hands when you can't."
—Mark Schultz

*T*ime froze, and all of a sudden, I gasped for air and felt a shiver go through my body. I was still here! Thank God I was still here!

I rushed upstairs from the basement in disbelief and ran out the front door, falling to the concrete steps for some fresh air. Images of my children flashed before my eyes—what would they have done without a mother? It was a chilling moment, and I cried out to the Lord and vowed to overcome bipolar disorder.

Something inside me changed as I realize that my actions were risky and reckless. Fortunately, Dr. Varra was at the office and we talked in person. Shortly thereafter, he made arrangements for another inpatient hospitalization and notified Derek.

The psych unit was dotted with familiar faces. Nurses and staff noticed a faint sparkle in my eyes instead of a death glare. While I sat alone in my room, many thoughts came to mind. The desire to get better was half the battle and a positive mindset was the other. I needed to find ways to adapt to *live* with the illness because it was never going to go away—but in time it could be managed.

After a twenty-four-hour suicide watch, I attended group therapy. The meeting room hadn't changed a bit, only the faces of the first-time patients who were terrified of the unknown. The look was all too familiar, and I understood. This time I wasn't shy and started a conversation, hoping to set aside their anxieties. Could I be a light in their darkness? Then it clicked again.

Bipolar meets God. I was alive, and I could share my story with others. The thought gave me a sense of purpose. I still had a voice and would use it to share with others about bipolar disorder and God.

During my time in the unit I found ownership, belonging, and *acceptance* for the first time since the diagnosis and initial hospitalization. Somehow an internal burden was lifted. I really did have a lot to offer the world, especially those suffering with mental illness.

Later a young psychiatrist explained a new treatment approach and prescribed several medications to treat *each* symptom separately since there was no magic pill. But a stimulant was also added, which would help with concentration and combat chronic fatigue. If there was no response, ECTs (electroconvulsive treatments, also known as shock therapy) would be necessary as a last resort to treat the depression. The psychiatrist had a nearby office, so we would keep in touch through regular visits after dismissal. What great news to share with my family!

The reunion was bittersweet. Derek and the boys showered me with attention and I had never embraced them so tightly and so long. We caught up in the car while riding to the clinic for an appointment with my new counselor, Beth. Hopefully she would be more empathetic than a man.

The office was inviting and cozy. We talked openly as a family about the diagnosis, and Beth even read a picture book to the boys about a mommy with a mood disorder using childlike language so they could understand. She also took time to answer Michael's and Lukus's questions—and they no longer felt outside the box. Her approach was brilliant.

Also discussed were the wrap-around approach for my treatment and *relapse prevention.* Many adaptations were going to be made in the household and to our routine. Every member of the family had an important role in my *recovery.* The word was hopeful and positive!

One more step: Beth enrolled me in the community support program. A case worker assisted me with setting goals to improve living skills, medication compliance, budgeting, and identifying triggers. Better yet, she would make house calls. Derek and I had no idea such programs existed—and it made the homecoming more manageable.

An immaculate house awaited this time. Tiny hands pulled me into the corner of the living room, where there was a brand-new glider and ottoman. It would be perfect for rocking the blues away. And then another gift of bubble bath and scented lotions for a little aromatherapy.

Later in the evening the boys draped over my chest as we snuggled on the couch, just as they had done when they were babies and I could hear and feel their tiny heartbeats. I whispered, "Mommy's okay now." The moment could have lasted forever. Feeling alive and safe after a long period of darkness felt amazing. God was answering prayer.

Beth and I met for an hour each week for therapy. She offered a fresh perspective and reminded me that "bipolar" was not stamped on my forehead and I wasn't crazy or stupid. This was important encouragement for anyone suffering from a mental illness. It was like any other chronic lifetime illness. It was time for me to let go of the stigma and embrace the role of a mother since it was the most important job. Balancing it and quiet time was key. Beth suggested a support group.

Seated in the conference room were a handful of women, all of varying ages. They were eager to hear the new girl's story. They showed compassion and understanding, and I found a sense of belonging when they shared their diagnosis. After the group session, we continued our conversation at a nearby restaurant. Peer support made all the difference. We found friendship, understanding, and empathy.

During the next med check with Dr. Cheng, I reported adequate sleep and a decrease in cycling and its severity. He attributed it to the colorful capsules and tablets in my pill box. At times it was overwhelming to keep track of them all, but after three years of bouncing back and forth on meds, the right combination had been found. Better yet, the stimulant was a game-changer since it helped with focus and energy throughout the day no matter what the task. For the first time in three years, no adjustments were necessary—that was great news! I could concentrate on exploring new coping skills at home.

Housework didn't have to be daunting. Latin music was the best! I would sing along to Enrique, dance the cha-cha in the kitchen, and jive while folding laundry. The upbeat tempo kept me moving along throughout the afternoon, and I was mentally refreshed for the boys when they came home after school.

I enjoyed the fresh air while waiting for the school bus on the front steps. The boys raced down the driveway with their backpacks flopping, which were just as big as they were. My eyes sparkled like diamonds as they jumped into my lap and told me about their day, all while I was thinking, *This is what being a mother is all about!* The simplest moments were the most precious, especially since I was finally stable and healthy.

The school year flew by. At semester's end I attended parent-teacher conferences. Lukus was a straight-A student and loved helping others in class. Michael did well too but was having attention and sensory issues that needed to be addressed by an occupational therapist.

A team of caring professionals met with us for his individualized education plan and discussed strategies, including the wrap-around approach, just like my own treatment plan. I gave a plethora of information and suggestions. It felt good to be heard.

God certainly had a plan. Had it not been for the bipolar, I might not have been able to advocate for Michael. The teachers were kind in their compliments about my wellness and progress. My diagnosis was never kept a secret.

An agency representative, Jessica, interviewed us in our home so they could understand our specific needs as a family and set up a game plan. She assisted with organization, mapping out daily tasks, coordinating appointments, and placing important reminders on the fridge. Everything was falling into place. Taking care of my family was easier.

When spring rolled around, many parents volunteered for field trips. While riding the bus to the zoo with Lukus, I looked around and felt a sense of belonging with the other mommies. And at the end of the school year he brought *me* for a show-and-tell and proudly said, "Hi. This is my mom," leaving me feeling like a million dollars, and it seemed the bipolar disorder didn't exist at all. Balance had been found. We began counting down the last of the school days.

Derek and I had a surprise for the boys—a weekend at our favorite place at a lake. The lake was serene and a place of relaxation, where we breathed in the fresh air and set up the tents and got our campsite in order. Then we started a fire and roasted hobos and hot dogs and made a pot of beanie weenie surprise. What camping trip would be complete without a s'more or two?

At dusk Derek and the boys lined up their lawn chairs alongside the river with their fishing poles dangling and waited to hear the bells of the catfish hunter. It was a picture-perfect moment.

Late into the evening we retired for the night, zipped up our sleeping bags, and drifted off to sleep. No one ever knew that I awoke in the middle of the night and stood outside the tent and stared up at the moon and the stars and all their wonder. Maybe, just maybe there was a place for me in the world. *Bipolar meets God.* The journey was just beginning.

CHAPTER 7

Ending a Marriage

"I know the plans I have for you," declares the Lord, "plans to prosper you and not harm you, plans to give you hope and a future."
—Jeremiah 29:11

"All I've got is hurt and these four words: Thy will be done."
—Hillary Scott & The Scott Family

A remarkable view of the backyard could be seen from the picture window next to the dining room table and chairs, which were made of oak and had held up for generations. It was a place to gather for meals, celebrations, and everyday conversation. But over time it became a place of blame, anger, and frustration.

The clock tick-tocked into the night while I waited for Derek. My mind was racing. Was he still mad from last night's fight? Was he coming home at all? The sound of him at the door set aside my worries—until he walked in without a word and retreated to the office. His rejection was painful, and I went to bed alone again, pondering many what-ifs.

The next day the boys and I pulled out the wedding album, beautifully engraved and made of heavy leather. We took a seat at the kitchen table and looked at it page by page. They were surprised to see how young Mommy and Daddy once were.

In one photo Derek and I were facing each other on the sidewalk next to the church. My veil, his cowboy hat, one precious moment caught forever. Although it was our favorite photo, I barely recognized the bride and groom anymore, and it brought mixed emotions. Eighteen years together had weathered us through life's storms. Our marriage was full of secrets behind closed doors, and we drifted farther apart. Like other couples, because of our children Derek and I weren't ready to give up yet. Perhaps therapy would help put us back together.

Tim, a certified counselor, looked distinguished in his tie and sweater vest and led us to a comfortable office with leather chairs and offered us a cup of coffee. We talked openly about our marital concerns. Within minutes Derek and I began arguing. Tim shook his head.

"Sorry, guys. We're not going to play the blame game or point fingers. We're here to find out what your issues are and how to address them." Then he asked a big question: "Have you two thought about divorce?" Silence. "Let's try to change that over the coming weeks."

Forty-five minutes passed by quickly each week as Derek and I discussed each other's concerns and reviewed assignments. Honesty was important.

Tim had some great ideas for us to ponder. How did we communicate? Did we share emotions with one another? Did we spend quality time together without the boys? Derek and I almost simultaneously said, "*What* alone time—with two young boys?" We faced the harsh reality that intimacy barely existed, and there was no quality alone time anymore. Tim suggested a weekend getaway, and Derek took care of planning it. His parents were eager to watch the boys.

At the campground we enjoyed fishing by the lakeside, which reminded us of our honeymoon as we hoped to rekindle a smidgen of our love. But a storm moved in, and it poured for two days, so we stayed inside the small camper and got on each other's nerves. Derek decided to cut the trip short, and I mastered the art of nitpicking for the hour-long drive.

Back at home, Derek unloaded the camper while I tucked the boys into their beds. Back in the kitchen Derek made snide comments, and so did I. It escalated, and in a moment of anger Derek pushed me up against the hutch and raised his hand. That had never happened before. It was scary. A line had been crossed, and it could never be taken away. Derek left quickly and sped away into the night.

The boys were in the hallway crying. I realized they had gotten out of bed, had seen the scuffle, and were afraid too. It was a painful moment as a mother, and I sensed there was going to be a dramatic change in our lives.

Morning came. Derek was gone, so I slipped out of bed and put on a pot of coffee and woke the boys up. They scuttled to the TV with their blankets and watched cartoons while munching on Pop-Tarts. This was a good time to call my father.

He already knew the marriage was in trouble for a long time, and wasn't surprised when I asked him to help with legal fees, not having any resources of my own. Of course, he was willing to do anything to help his daughter. It was time to let go of the marriage. Dad reminded me of the promise of Romans 8:28, which took me back to the brave girl on Senior Sunday. She was fearless and had looked at the world with big, open eyes.

In the bedroom I gathered my thoughts while sitting on the bed, then pulled back the rose-colored drapes and stared out the window for the longest time. Was there a better life out there? A peaceful sensation came over me, and knowing it came from God, I picked up the dusty Bible off the headboard and prayed: *Heavenly Father, it's been a long time since I've talked to you. I'm afraid. I don't think I* can stay in this marriage anymore. We have been together for a long time—and he's all I know. How could I ever exist without him or make it on my own? But I'm so tired of fighting. And he got so angry. The boys can't be around this. I can't be around this. I have to leave. Please help me through this and give me strength.

God had never left my side, even when I didn't attend church or pray regularly. The anxiety subsided because a decision had been made. I exhaled a sigh of relief as God filled me with an abundance of hope, courage, and strength. The answer was clear, and there was much planning to do.

I met with a local attorney and signed legal documents, including a petition for divorce, which was filed with the district court later that same afternoon. I was the plaintiff. Derek was the defendant, and it made him angry, although we agreed that divorce was the only option. When he came home from work he waved the papers in the air and told me I would feel his wrath—whatever that meant.

Although there was intense animosity between us, we *had* to find common ground so we could tell the boys about the divorce. We prayed they would understand.

At the dining room table we gathered for pizza, cheesy breadsticks, root beer, and dessert. The boys gobbled it up and drank their root beer. Michael let out a loud burp and laughed—well, we all did. Normally he would be scolded, but it put us all at ease.

"Boys, listen closely. Mommy and Daddy love you very much. We have decided to get a divorce. That means we won't be married anymore and will live separately. You'll live here with Daddy, and you'll also live with me. I'll move at the end of summer. This is not your fault."

Lukus looked at us with his big blue eyes. "Does that mean you and Daddy aren't going to fight anymore?"

The way he said it could make any parent cry. But it was also proof that children see and hear more than we think they do. I felt

Ending a Marriage

sad and relieved all at the same time—and very proud of them for listening so closely. Now it was Derek's turn to talk.

"Boys, this will be difficult for us all. Let's try to remember the good times. Tonight let's make it about you. We're going to go to the theater!"

They jumped and hollered. "We *never* go to the movies! *Transformers!*"

Derek and I couldn't afford to take them very often, but we wanted to make them feel special. During our time together watching the big screen and eating popcorn there was a sense of bonding even in the midst of a life-changing decision.

We confided in the neighbor couple about the divorce. They offered many solutions and support and lent us a copy of the Christian movie *Fireproof*. Although we connected to its meaning and cried, it was simply too late for a reconciliation. Besides, we were knee-deep in the legal process. The wedge between us was growing.

We were at the mercy of our attorneys. Do this, say that, track this, note that. It brought out the worst in us. Derek and I had been together for eighteen years and now could hardly be in the same room without tearing each other down. One day the boys got caught in the crossfire. They were never meant to hear grown-up words that should never be spoken in the first place. To comfort them, we brought them into the bedroom every night until moving day.

The California King could still easily fit four, and by morning we were all tangled up with one another—moments of relative peace as our time as a family was coming to an abrupt end. This brought mixed emotions.

The boys and I drove to town to look at an apartment. It wasn't a coincidence when a song from *Fireproof* played over the radio. Crumble. Fade. Our marriage hadn't fallen apart overnight. Ten years, two years, six months? It was impossible to pinpoint when the breakdown had started. Many what-if's came to mind as we pulled up to the brick triplex.

The landlord, a pretty petite woman, gave us a tour. It was nice! The boys bounced from room to room and were amused at the small space, the "tiny house," as they called it. The 900-square-foot apartment was perfect, although the price was a bit steep for my limited budget. God would make a way.

Back at home, packing continued. Michael and Lukus earned a few dollars by carrying up boxes from the basement. As the days passed, physical and mental exhaustion set in to the point of giving up, so I lay down on the bed to rest. Lukus stumbled in, hopped up onto the bed, and gave me a picture.

"Mommy, look. What do the footprints and the beach mean?" he asked.

"It's a very special poem. Let me read it to you." He listened intently and I hoped he understood its meaning. "Why don't we hang this in your new bedroom?" I asked. It was a timeless reminder from God in the moment.

Both boys dealt with the divorce in different ways. Lukus slept with the dogs underneath the oak table. To him it was a safe place, where Tiger and Blue Puppy, his favorite stuffed animals, kept watch. Michael, however, was "tougher" and had fits of anger, taking refuge in the basement playing video games. But neither of them cried or complained. At times I couldn't believe the divorce was actually happening. Maybe second thoughts were normal.

One Friday morning Derek and I sat at the table. Derek spoke after moments of silence. "You know, Kristi, think about how many times we've sat here. This was Grandpa and Grandma's. Remember all the cookies and coffee?" I nodded—those were special times. "Are you sure this is what you want?" *Were we doing the right thing?* There were many reasons to stay, but there were more reasons to leave.

How could we ever go back? Too many things had been said and done during the legal process. Suddenly, according to him, bipolar disorder supposedly made me an unfit mother, and I fired back about his drinking. But if we didn't agree, the judge would decide where the boys would live. Neither of us wanted that. Maybe it was better for Derek and me to ignore each other and let the attorneys referee. Moving day couldn't come soon enough.

Dad arrived with the trailer hooked up to his Ford. Derek studied every box that left the house and asked one redundant question: "You don't have any of *my* stuff, do you?"

I didn't take much of anything, only personal belongings and a couple of end tables and the glider rocker because he didn't allow me to take much, not even a single piece of silverware. That gave new meaning to starting over in every sense.

While we carried the last box to the car, our shoulders brushed up against each other, and then I handed him the house keys. Thirteen years of marriage came to an end, and neither of us could show any emotion. But a piece of my heart was breaking because I still loved him, and also because I wouldn't see the boys every day anymore. That was the worst part of the divorce, so I hugged them extra-long and tightly as I said goodbye.

While looking at the picture-perfect house, I could still see them chasing me with garter snakes in the rain. Nothing felt better than the wet grass and mud between our toes and the laughter that came with it. As with any mother, they were my world, and it didn't matter where we called home as long as we were together.

CHAPTER 8

New Beginnings

*Shout for joy to God, all the earth! Sing the glory
of his name; make his praise glorious.*
—Psalm 66:1–2

"He is."
—Mark Schultz

A powerful Christian song played on the radio and brings comfort as I traveled along the highway, which was similar to life with its twists and turns and my lack of knowledge of what was ahead. One thing was for sure–God *was* with me, especially while starting a new life.

As I parked the car, a surge of emotions fell over me for many reasons. How long had it been since I lived on my own? Could I handle all the responsibility? It was important to remember that God brought the boys and me to this location for a reason. The apartment was just blocks away from downtown, the grandparents, friends, and the Methodist church.

All of my worldly belongings fit into a small corner opposite the living room. The empty apartment didn't bring sadness but rather a sense of pride. I stretched out on the thin, beige carpet and prayed for courage and strength in the midst of new beginnings. The rest of the afternoon was spent running errands downtown, later returning mid-afternoon to unpack. Dad's vintage Panasonic radio kept me company into the late morning hours until I crashed on the bedroom floor with a blanket.

At first light came the aroma of coffee. Dad was an early riser and at the front door. He was ready to unload the living room furniture off the trailer. We had quite a time carrying the couch down the narrow stairwell. Despite our best efforts, it was not going to fit. So much for a matching set. Maybe we could find a garage sale or two to fill in the gaps.

Lucky for us, we found a large estate sale, where we bought an 80s wooden dinette set, a hutch, and some mattresses for the boys. Dad and I rode back to the apartment, unloaded the furniture, and then he put my bed together. It was starting to look like home! We joked about our cheap finds. Our giggles were honest and lighthearted. As we said goodbye, I truly realized how important he was. Dad would do anything for his family. God was providing an opportunity for us to become even closer.

I headed back out to scope the neighborhood and came upon some mismatched pieces of furniture. The man took five dollars for all of them and even offered to deliver them to the apartment. The microwave cart would make a great nightstand—all it needed was a little tender loving care. God provided in the most simple ways.

Friends and family called throughout the week. "How is moving going? How are the boys?" Then Sis called. She was an ordained pastor of a United Methodist church about sixty miles away. She reminded me that one of her colleagues who lived in our town was going to stop by in the evening.

A slender woman in her fifties with a brown bob stood the door. "Hi—you must be Kristi. My name is Eleanor. I'm the associate pastor at the United Methodist Church here in York. Welcome to the neighborhood. I live just down the street in the parsonage. Is this a good time to visit?" It was nice to meet someone new.

She was lovely and kind. Eleanor shared her story, which put me at ease, so much in fact that I told her all the details about my bipolar disorder and divorce—and also confessed my long absence from church and the shame it brought. Pastor Eleanor was nonjudgmental and offered reassurance, extending an invitation to service on Sunday. And before leaving, she prayed for me. *How long had it been since someone did that for me?*

At bedtime the bed was a cozy place to read my new study Bible. In the background the Christian radio station played a familiar tune. Why was I hearing it so often? No coincidence at all, really. God was speaking to my broken heart than needed mending. Someday there would be an understanding of the pain experienced in the midst of divorce. God heard every bedtime prayer.

The sound of little feet marched down the stairwell. Thump, thump, thump, thump. The boys burst into the apartment and ran straight to their new bedroom. Cool!" said Michael. "Little beds on the floor!"

To them it was fun and they didn't notice an absence of traditional box springs as the mattresses sat on shabby metal frames. The white plastic shelves would do for their clothes until I could afford dressers. The boys gave a quick look at the rest of the apartment and noticed a brand-new washer and dryer in the utility room, a gift from dad so we didn't have to go to the laundromat across town.

There was one more surprise in the garage. Grandpa enjoyed fixing up old bicycles and left two of them in the garage. The brothers hooted and hollered as they put on their helmets and went for a quick ride around the block. Oh, the places they could go!

In the afternoon we walked along the charming brick streets of downtown and noticed the historic buildings, including the opera house, which was home to a variety of stores, beauty parlors, boutiques, and eateries, maybe a legendary bakery too, a skip past the supermarket and also the movie theater that Big Grandpa used to manage in the late sixties. The town square had it all!

The spacious consignment shop on the corner had anything for anyone. Lukus found a trio of bean bags, so we bought them and carried them home—what a sight! Then sirens blared, so we rushed across the street and watched the ladder truck roll out. Who doesn't want to be a hero? Michael was smitten and vowed to be a fireman when he grew up.

New beginnings meant new traditions in the tiny apartment, which included baking the first of many homemade meals. We snuggled close together on the loveseat for pan pizza and a movie—that was one tradition to keep.

At bedtime we gathered in the corner by the glider rocker in our pajamas. The boys shared their feelings about the divorce, particularly about living in two homes—it wasn't easy. Reading from the Bible gave them comfort, so much, in fact, that they pleaded for more. The words of Psalm 142 and 143 were just what we needed to hear. *I cry aloud to the Lord. . . Lord, hear my prayer* (Psalm 142:1; 143:1). Lukus thanked me for introducing him to God. What mother wouldn't shed tears?

To ease the first-night jitters, the boys took their pillows and blankets to the master bedroom floor—Tiger and Blue Puppy too. After they fell asleep, I took a photo of them and later framed and placed it on the windowsill. There was never going to be a day when I didn't say goodnight to them in my own way.

The next morning Dad arrived. The boys were in their Sunday best and ran to him, bragging about their clip-on ties. "Don't we look snazzy?" exclaimed Lukus. The boys noticed my new dress. When your children say you are pretty, believe them! It was a great day to worship together.

The church was a historical beauty, built in the 1800s. The sanctuary was spectacular with its red carpet and pews throughout, and the stained-glass windows were the most beautiful we had ever seen, especially the one on the south side. Dad guided us to a pew near the altar. The moment was emotional, and I whispered, "I'm home," as we took our seats.

The pastors walked down the aisle wearing traditional robes and took their places at the lecterns. The service was much like that of my childhood, with the singing of hymns, an anthem by the choir, and readings from the Bible. But it also included a praise-and-worship team that featured traditional and contemporary Christian songs. We sang a popular song also heard on the radio—it had such an important message for the beginning of our new life. The song would have significant meaning later on down the road.

As the offering plate was passed, Michael's and Lukus's faces lit up as they each put a dollar bill in it. Standing and singing the doxology reminded us of our deep family Methodist roots that stretched out for seven generations. The Spirit moved through my body and soul, a magnificent feeling. At last, new beginnings with God and the church were taking place. After the benediction, everyone joined hands while singing the final song. There was a sense of belonging and it felt wonderful.

The congregation was friendly, especially the three elderly ladies who sat behind us and a handful of members who reached out to say hello before we said goodbye. One man, robust in size and in generous nature, leaned in for a half-hug. Dad smiled at us and put his hands over his heart. How proud he was to have his daughter and grandsons back in church!

It seemed as if I never took a pause from church at all, and I vowed right then and there never to miss a Sunday, not ever, and to pray faithfully, especially since there were many struggles ahead.

The courtroom was just as intimidating as the judge. Derek and I stood before him along with our attorneys and waited for the custody ruling. I almost collapsed when he awarded Derek temporary physical custody. *I* was a stay-at-home mother. *I* knew all their habits. *I* was always there for them while he worked second shift. Derek's smirk angered me, but no emotion could be shown in the courtroom. Worse yet, another shock– *I* was ordered to pay child support to Derek until we went to trial in eight long months. It wasn't until then that the judge would make a ruling on permanent custody and child support.

Every payment was made early via certified mail so he couldn't complain. After the dust settled, we agreed to spend time equally with the boys—nights included. I underestimated the hurt I experienced by not seeing them every day. Dad and I became closer. He was very supportive. We had long conversations on the phone every day, even late in the evening when worry got the best of me. How would I ever pay child support, let alone money for rent, utilities, and food? Dad reminded me that he *could* help but encouraged me to pinch pennies to become more independent in the long run. Certainly going without wasn't a big deal—and the coins would eventually add up. Dad always gave good advice and reminded me that we could visit anytime.

Getting out of the apartment to visit with Dad would do the boys and me good, so I decided to do it. The hour-long drive was a breeze, and we left right after school on Friday. It would be a fun getaway.

The townhome had a spare room with a comfy bed and a cot. The bedding was a mixture of new and very old. The blue floral sheets had to have been on my childhood bed! They were comforting and familiar at the moment. We freshened up for a minute, and then Dad took us to his favorite Mexican restaurant. Can you believe he had been dining there since 1976? The Eagle's Club provided Friday night entertainment. A live country-Western band was featured. Dad and I twirled around the dance floor for what seemed like hours but also two-stepped, honky-tonked, and waltzed. It was fun to teach the boys a line dance, but they had two left feet. Maybe next time.

Back at the townhome a bedtime snack of milk and Oreos brought smiles and sweet dreams to sleepy eyes. Dad and I talked well past midnight. He was becoming my best friend and confidant. Oh, how he loved the Lord and his family, always loving, kind, and generous! He was a wonderful role model.

At the crack of dawn we had plate-sized pancakes for all at a nearby diner. While sipping coffee, I chuckled, noticing the similar mannerisms and physical features of a grandpa and his grandsons.

We then putted around in dad's Smurf-blue Ford on the lookout for garage sales and wondered what bargains could be found for the apartment or for Dad's growing collections of "double-tapered left-handed mckiddling pins for a canoodling" valves—that's what he called them!

Then we browsed a long line of consignment shops, many of which had upscale clothes, shoes, and more. Dad told us to load up since the bill was on him. He made us feel special and loved.

At the townhome we took a tour of Grandpa's basement, filled with collections of knives, canes, and tools of any nature, plus gizmos and gadgets, tinkers and tankets. Oh, how Grandpa loved telling stories about all of them!

Then a lesson in the garage. Dad showed the boys how to change the oil, put air in the tires, and look underneath the hood of my car. For helping, they each received a ten-dollar bill. Their eyes lit up. That was a lot of money! A multitude of toys and candy could be found at the dollar store. Dad handed me something, too–an envelope from the bank. I sighed and pushed it away. "I'll be okay, Dad. I don't need your help," I said.

"Kristi, I know you don't need to help but I *want* to help. Rat hole this. You'll need it sometime. You're a good mom and you're living the right kind of life"—which meant living a godly life and attending church faithfully. His generosity was appreciated. We gave him a small sign we had found downtown: *DAD'S GARAGE. OIL*

CHANGES ALWAYS FREE. He put it up that instant on the wall. The true meaning behind it brought tears. Then we got into our car and drove out of the private cul-de-sac.

The old Bonneville had nearly 200,000 miles on it from endless trips between Derek's house and mine. During the twenty-minute drive I turned the radio off because it was a perfect time to talk to God.

In the car the brothers shared all the happenings in their father's home. I didn't need to know *everything*, but listened and took it with a grain of salt.

Back at home they threw their bookbags onto the floor and grabbed granola bars as they ran out the front door. "Put on your coats!" I yelled, but every Midwestern kid seemed to be immune to the cold. It was already November. The only thing that would stop them on their bicycles was the snow and ice—winter weather would come at any time.

Three cooks in the crowded kitchen stirred up love, new recipes, and memories! Who could forget Lukus's cheesy garlic ritzas or Michael's Boy Scout pizzas? Four-pack biscuit tubes had endless possibilities. We didn't mind eating cheap, either—in fact, it became an art. Maybe they would be the next Emeril. Bam! Bam! Bam! And no worries—they made plenty of desserts. The lopsided angel food cake would never be forgotten—sweet smiles for the camera to remember the weekends that never lasted long enough.

When the boys returned to their dad's, I turned the furnace down to sixty-four degrees to save a few pennies. It was cold, but the eight blankets piled up on the bed kept me warm. The makeshift microwave night stand next to it doubled as a bookshelf. The top was cluttered in true Kristi Kay fashion.

Once I was under the covers, my Bible in hand, reading the Psalms gave me comfort, just as my sis said they would. Psalm 62 was a favorite and was highlighted it in a pretty shade of pink. I also reminisced about the many personal notes at the top of the page, which confirmed the start of a beautiful spiritual journey. I felt a strong sense of belonging with the Lord.

Glancing at Michael and Lukus's photos on the windowsill brought sadness. Missing them made our time more special. My heart ached for them.

I stopped by the church the next morning to speak with Pastor Eleanor, who led me into the dark sanctuary. Instead of sitting in a pew, we sat on the steps in front of the altar. God's light peeked through the magnificent windows.

"Look up, Kristi," she said as she pointed. "Look at the dove. If you feel afraid, just look at the dove and it will give you peace."

The Holy Spirit moved through my body and set my worries free. Pastor Eleanor understood the feeling wholeheartedly. Our chats were greatly appreciated, and she helped me navigate through a world of emotions and uncertainties during the divorce. Never once did she forget to pray for me. I would never forget the dove moment—in fact, it would prepare me for something greater.

Saturdays were spent gathering around the table for a simple meal followed by a game of Monopoly. A roll of the dice, pass go, and collect two hundred dollars. Just as it was underway, the doorbell rang. Michael raced to see who it was.

Standing there was a man holding a box of food. He was from the church across town. Surely he had the wrong address, but he reassured us that our family was nominated for a Thanksgiving basket. Someone cared about us. We had never experienced such generosity and thanked him many times. We were eager to see what was inside.

Together the boys carried the box into the kitchen. In it was a turkey and all the trimmings. "Look at all the food, Mom!" they said in unison. "It's gonna be go-od!"

On Thanksgiving Day we cooked a feast together and served it on Grandmother's porcelain china. We picked every last bit of meat off the turkey for leftovers all week. Little hands fought over the wishbone. For dessert we had pecan pie, all the while sharing blessings.

Dad dropped off a funny little Charlie Brown Christmas tree over the weekend, and we decorated it with homemade grade school ornaments—gingerbread men, clothespin reindeers, and candy canes. We had stockings, lights, and Great-Grandpa's 1943 copy of *The Night Before Christmas.*

Dad was also thoughtful enough to bring wrapped gifts for the boys to put under the tree, knowing I had money enough only for stocking-stuffers. He understood the true meaning of Christmas and never asked for anything in return except two happy boys on Christmas morning. *But what he had done for me?* It was hard to put into words. Part of my heart was changed forever.

The Advent season was magical—the church sanctuary was adorned with trees, lights, and wreaths. And on the altar was the nativity scene. Singing hymns with my sons was precious since they could experience Christ as I did as a child. It was great to be back *home*—in many ways.

Before service one Sunday the pastor asked for a moment of my time. In his hands was an envelope with a cash donation from an anonymous member who wanted to help give the boys a good Christmas. "I couldn't," I said. But after a short pause I accepted it, believing that someday God would provide so that I could pay it forward. Pastor promised to share my gratitude with the giver. Inside the envelope was two hundred dollars!

The boys raced home on the sidewalk. While walking out of the church, a middle-aged woman stopped me. "I'm so happy to see you and your boys in church, always looking so nice. Old-school Methodist, right?" Then she handed me some cash and whispered, "Please use this for Christmas gifts." I burst into tears while thanking her.

Between the two cash gifts, there was four hundred dollars total!

Imagine how far that much money could go for a single mother. I looked up at God and said, "Why me?"

The boys and I gathered for a chat. Attending church was important and we now had an extended family who cared about us, a kind of love we had never experienced before. Surprisingly, the boys understood the general meaning of kindness and compassion since there was a clothing drive at school for families less fortunate.

School was dismissed for holiday break two weeks later—and just in time. The snow fell heavily and fast as we pulled into the garage. After a bowl of chili and monkey bread, we bundled up and made the best snowman in town and didn't finish it until after dark. We took a photograph to remember the big snowstorm.

By morning over a foot of snow covered the ground, enough to slide down the town's big hill on saucers and toboggans—until little fingers and toes had turned red, wet, and cold. But a cup of hot cocoa would remedy that!

A knock at the door. The kind, robust man from church was holding a large box of food—a gift from a private club for their annual Christmas food drive. How could we be so blessed to receive such a bountiful gift again? The feeling was overwhelming.

A generous-sized ham, canned goods, and bags of apples, oranges, and potatoes covered the table, including two bags of Brach's holiday candy. It was an overwhelming moment because people *noticed* us. People *cared* about us. Being a single mom on a tight budget, I was so grateful, and the gift of food and a holiday meal was priceless. God had provided again. With Him anything is possible.

At bedtime Lukus found a tiny white feather stuck in the carpet where we gathered to pray. "Mom, where did this come from?" he asked. There was no logical explanation, other than the obvious to a believer. I taped the feather in my Bible and made a note: "Feathers, small, dainty feathers, appear in our home as if angels were here watching and protecting. And a little reminder was left behind saying, "We are watching over you. You have a guardian angel, and I'm here for you."

I truly believed in angels. To a seven- and nine-year-old, it was majestic and gave me an opportunity to talk about the miracle of Baby Jesus, which is the greatest privilege of a mother.

The church sanctuary and its balcony were packed full of familiar faces on Christmas Eve. Beautiful hymns, holy Communion, and singing "Silent Night" by candlelight were just what our hearts needed. The spirit of Christ's birth and my babes closely nestled beside me brought extraordinary delight.

The moonlight paved the way in the darkness as we stomped through the snow. Lukus lay on the ground to make a snow angel while Michael stuck his tongue out to catch the heavy, wet snowflakes. I experienced moments of peace, contentment, and simple joy just watching them.

Another foot of snow welcomed Christmas morning. Two excited boys dragged me into the living room, where they ripped open the presents: Transformers, toys, and also much-needed clothing and socks. In two remaining boxes were expensive jeans and shirts from the school's clothing drive, which brought mixed emotions. It was okay that others helped. I was doing the best I could.

My only gifts to the boys were stocking-stuffers and gift bags, each with a box of brownie mix and a bottle of sarsaparilla, which became a tradition for years to come. Then we prayed and gave thanks for the many caring people who had made it the most meaningful Christmas ever.

Holidays were especially memorable the first year in the apartment. We were blessed by the ashes on Ash Wednesday, and then on Sunday we dressed in our finest. Just before service, a kind, robust man said, "You're a beautiful young lady." It was then that I realized *beautiful* had many meanings. My love for the Lord must have been obvious. He made me feel precious and beloved, and I would never forget his words.

Worship was *amazing*, especially the hymns: *Christ the Lord is risen today! Alleluia!* The boys and I were joyful to be back at church. My spirit never felt more alive!

The days became warmer, and finally hints of summer were all around, from freshly planted gardens to kids playing outside in the neighborhoods. Michael, Lukus, and I made it through the thick of winter and through divorce's difficult journey. We could finally breathe.

The judge ruled on the property settlement and awarded me a small sum of alimony and an equalization payment. Derek and I agreed to share joint legal custody, so neither of us would pay child support. My eight-month obligation to him was terminated. The divorce was final. Derek and I could finally move on with our lives—and just in time for summer.

I popped over one day to chat with the neighbor lady, Bethany. She was just as sweet as her ever-blooming flower garden. Michael and Lukus buzzed down the hill on their bicycles. They had just been at Beaver Creek and had surprises in their backpacks. Bethany laughed because she was a retired teacher and knew firsthand the mischief boys get into.

Michael pulled out a snapping turtle and had to show us its many tricks. When he stood up, golf balls fell from his backpack onto the ground and rolled away. He scurried to get them because he could sell them and make money. "Anything else?" I asked, laughing.

"Look, Mommy. More rocks for my collection," said Lukus as he laid them on the front steps. He was adding to what his great grandpa started generations ago. Then he dug for more in his front pocket, which yielded an old bottle cap embedded in a piece of chewed-up bubble gum. "Oops—sorry, Mommy." His innocence was amusing. Their grand adventures would be halted in a short time when we visited the city's outdoor pool and aquatic center.

Opening day was a perfect eighty-five degrees and not a cloud in the sky. We laid our beach towels on the loungers. The boys put on their goggles, jumped into the water, splashed around, and then played on the floating dragon. It was going to be a great summer! Every day Michael and Lukus gained confidence and perfected their form when diving off the board, with maybe an occasional backflip for show!

The designated lap lane was divine. It was a place to trim down and tone up and reminded me of my good old swim team days. When a break was needed, I called Michael and Lucus over to the snack bar, where Chaco tacos melted in their hands as the hot sun beat down.

An entourage of boys arrived, best friends from down the block. Together they were courageous enough to check out the monster slide, where screams turned into giggles. At the hoop a thriving basketball game in the water took place before testing out the new rock wall. Good times for all.

The sun kissed my beautifully tanned body. Gliding through the water was so calming, as if my bipolar disorder didn't exist at all. Another added benefit was a slimmer figure. The boys and I didn't want summer to end.

At least there was one more night to enjoy the pool at the midnight swim. Under the bright lights, the boys and their preteen posse splished and splashed to the blaring music. With their neon glow sticks, they jived, dived, jumped, and flipped in the air, doing cannonballs too. Who could make the biggest splash? They were all winners in my book.

One particular evening the three of us followed the trails around town under a full moon–it must have put a spell on them. They shared all their stories, secrets, and confessions with their trusted girly-girly mom and even welcomed advice. I took a photograph of them in the heart of downtown to remember the moment. My heart burst with love.

After we had been in the apartment one year, a celebration

was in order. We had so much to be grateful for. I felt particularly accomplished having mastered the art of budgeting. The boys were fully aware of our financial situation. It was simple, really. Living on a cash-only basis was one of the best life lessons that could be taught. Being thrifty wasn't a bad thing.

We would made a loop around town in the car to the various second-hand stores. Ten for ten at Goodwill, ninety-nine-cent spectacular on the corner, and round the bend, our favorite thrift shop, where an employee would hand us three sacks to fill for only five dollars each! It was a fun treasure hunt. Then we would make one last stop at the library for free books of any nature. Back at home the boys would curl up on the bean bags with their new reads.

For a special weekend splurge, we took a shopping trip to the discount stores in the city. Watching them pick out their own clothes brought smiles, especially since they were coming of age. Lukus always picked out a few extras since he was a good sport about his big brother's hand-me-downs. As we checked out, the full cart brought a sigh of relief as I remembered the times the cart was mostly empty. It took time, but with God's help we had come so far!

The brothers high-fived as we walked into the theater. In all the years, we never missed a Marvel comic movie. This time we saw it on the big screen in reclining seats and enjoyed endless buckets of buttered popcorn and soda pop. Even a simple outing meant the world to us, because we couldn't do it often.

Sunday morning after worship service, a potluck dinner took place in the fellowship hall. It was the only place to find one hundred different dishes under the same roof! Members called us by name. Pastor Don sat down to chat and noted our perfect attendance and strong faith. He invited me to give a short testimony of faith for the upcoming capital campaign. I was honored, having waited thirty years for His calling. The church gave us a sense of belonging and a place to call home.

The church garden was a perfect place to sit and meditate. Looking up at the wooden cross took me back to my childhood, and I instinctively hummed the beloved song from memory: *So I'll cherish the old rugged cross, / Till my trophies at last I lay down. / I will cling to the old rugged cross, / And exchange it someday for a crown.* Oh, how I loved the Lord, and He always provided. The testimony would be easy if I just spoke from the heart, and I bowed my head.

Just as I finished praying, the brothers rolled up on their bikes. The most interesting place to be was at the brook fishing from a handmade pole. One could find a multitude of treasures in the murky water. And they smelled like it too. I chuckled at the muddy footprints all the way down the stairwell. Don't get mad— just don't buy white socks anymore! Being their mother was my greatest joy!

On Sunday morning while standing in front of the congregation, I shared my strict Methodist upbringing and went on to describe how God had restored my life, including some details about the struggles of the divorce and being a single mother. There was no judgment—all the members had caring faces and listened intently.

I thanked the praise-and-worship team since I connected to God through song, a big part of my spiritual journey. I thanked the congregation for their love and support, then paid homage to my father, who was sitting in the pew between Michael and Lukus. It was a special moment I would always remember, especially since everyone saw the bright and shiny Kristi Kay, a woman of God, happy and full of life. When they applauded, it felt humbling and a fire inside reignited.

After the service a woman in her sixties with fur stole and painted lips introduced herself. "Hi. My name is Charlotte. You really shined up there, dear." There was an instant connection and we agreed to continue the conversation another day at a coffee shop, where Charlotte and I talked for hours about our families and our mutual love of fashion. It was a part of me forgotten in the busyness of raising boys. I felt brave enough to tell her about my bipolar disorder. She was surprised and wanted to know more about it and my spiritual journey. Kristi Kay finally had someone to talk to! Charlotte was a light in my darkness and became the girly friend I had never had. Maybe she was an angel sent from God. To find someone who understood my journey—priceless! We promised to get together regularly.

During lunch months later Charlotte noticed dark circles under my eyes and asked if I had been sick. Not really, just unusually tired. Keeping up with the boys was a challenge, and the chronic fatigue worsened, so a visit to my physician's assistant was necessary. She discovered a lower-than-normal heart rate, called bradycardia.

My doctor sent me to a cardiologist in the city, who ordered a battery of tests, but he was dissuaded due to my history with bipolar disorder, believing it was all "in my head." Months later came a second opinion, and then I underwent month-long cardiac monitor testing. The cardiologist was flabbergasted with the results. My heart rate was falling dangerously low during the overnight hours, especially at such a young age. Pacemaker surgery was scheduled immediately.

When I woke up, my family was right there, and the boys thought the new gadget was cool since their mother was now part machine, like their Transformer toys. The gray in my face disappeared almost immediately, and although a bit sore, I felt stronger. And just two days later, Michael and Lukus escorted me to church, where I gave thanks for the gift of life during the joys and concerns. God had mended my broken heart in multiple ways.

Despite celebrating my birthday on the mend, it was the best ever. The boys pulled me into the kitchen. "Look, Mommy. We made you chocolate chip *pan*cakes. Lukus always said it with enthusiasm. The dripping syrup everywhere brought only giggles. As we sat around the table, Michael presented me with a card and gift, wrapped up in a large towel. It was really heavy—what could it be? I was now the proud owner of a ginormous cardiac physiology book! They must have sneaked that one from the library.

The colder temperatures returned and brought us back indoors for the winter. On one occasion while at a friend's house, the boys played a guitar for the first time and dreamed of becoming the next country stars. On the drive home, "It's a Great Day to Be Alive," by Travis Tritt, played over the radio. God was reminding us how wonderful life was. We didn't need a lot of money or the best of things—we only needed to be together.

The following summer brought a simple vacation. We stayed at "Hotel Dad" and followed the creek behind the townhome, which led to a small pond, where the boys skipped rocks until dusk. The next day we visited the outdoor pavilion, where there was a traveling carnival. Two brothers braved the Tilt-A-Whirl, Sizzler, and Octopus. Once tummies quit fluttering, we dined at the newest eatery in town.

The next day we were off to Grandma's. We drove north to a state recreation park, where we enjoyed a picnic lunch, paddle boating at the marina, and climbing a tower to see for miles at the top. The trip couldn't be complete without a visit to the air and space museum. Who could forget the helicopter simulator? Tummies were fluttering again. Then we returned to Grandma's home for a lengthy chat about our ancestors.

Upon our return home, the joy turned into sadness, and anxiety settled in. Derek would be picking the boys up in the morning for his two-week vacation time. It was a long time to be away from them and be alone in the apartment.

I walked three times per day to pass the time, reaching the opposite side of town, where there were big, expensive houses, fancy cars, and perfectly sculpted lawns. What was it like on the insides of those houses? The owners obviously had plenty of money and the finest furnishings. I had very little of value regarding material possessions.

Satan's lies made me question my own worth. He was right—I

couldn't even give my kids what they needed, let alone something new or nice.

Passing by a chapel brought me hope and peace of mind. Not working helped maintain the delicate balance of my bipolar disorder. He *always* made a way for me, *always*. True wealth was defined by my relationship with God, and quality time with my children was priceless. Being a stay-at-home mother was truly a luxury. But sometimes it was hard to overcome the feelings of having less.

To cope, I began writing prayers on index cards and placing them in a coffee can during moments of despair that brought me to my hands and knees—literally. I cried out to God and promised to trust His timing.

I immersed myself in the church and started becoming more active. Charlotte persuaded me to join her for the annual fundraiser, well-loved and supported by the United Methodist Women. The fellowship hall was decorated beautifully for the event. It was fancy too, with a catered meal and live auction. The church ladies remembered my testimony and were happy to see a young, strong-faithed woman at the event. I promised to sponsor a table in the future and help more in other ways, all of which would bring me closer to God.

I finally gave the apartment a makeover, starting with a new welcome sign on the door, and in the living room an eighties montage of Monte Carlo blue-and-pink-flowered wingback chair and actual *couch* for us on which to watch our new flat screen TV. In the opposite corner were a cherry wood desk and personal computer. Wouldn't it be neat to write a book someday? The top of it was covered with a collection of Methodist hymnals, Bibles, and a coffee mug filled with Hershey's kisses—the secret to good writing.

In the bedroom were brand-new platform beds with thick mattresses and matching bedspreads for two now-teenage boys who had two very different personalities.

Michael's side was a bit disheveled. He was like me, delightfully chaotic. For the spirited teen, a dream catcher on the wall and a collection of wolves were a reminder of his father: tall, dark, and handsome with a hint of a mustache. On his dresser were a boombox and stack of rap CDs. Michael hip-hopped to his own style.

Lukus's half was immaculate. A handful of unusual what-nots and garage sale finds filled his nightstand, and the bookshelf was packed with science books—secrets to the hows and whys of the imagination. The self-professed brainiac sported a myriad of eclectic logo tees, including his favorite lime green "mind over matter" that he wore every chance he could. Lukus was gentle and kind and taught anyone who would listen, even when his voice started to crack.

They shared their space quite well and enjoyed playing video games on the box TV. It was a place to kick back and relax, but also a private space just for them as they transitioned into young men.

The master suite was decorated in all things pink, fluff, and foo-foo. The reversible bedding could capture the right mood and the furry pillows screamed girl power and femininity. I could never have had a bedroom like that if I were still married!

One day I glanced at the pictures on the windowsill and then looked up at the wall, where a newly framed poster-sized portrait of Michael and Lukus hung. Where had the time gone? Tears fell from my eyes, only to be rescued by my firstborn, who was dangling a set of car keys. "Can we go for a test drive? he asked.

I had driven the white sedan for fifteen years and needed something more reliable, so I had purchased a new-to-us mountain green SUV. She was a beaut! Michael climbed in the driver's seat and buckled up. I looked at him lovingly as a mother does and couldn't believe he was fifteen! Down the street and lickety split—a flawless drive around town.

Lukus had a pan of Texas Style frito pie waiting for us when we arrived home. A game of Farkle brought us together to joke and talk candidly. It was my job to mold them and love them—the boys wouldn't be at home forever.

"Teenage" found Michael and Lukus. Mom wasn't the coolest person to hang out with anymore. They spent their time with their buddies and sat around the fire pit exchanging jokes, doing video game tricks, and giggling about girls, who they were starting to notice.

It was nice to unwind at home alone whether it was curling up on the couch to watch TV or just to sit in silence. And in these moments I truly enjoyed my singleness, because it allowed precious moments with God.

One evening I dug under the bed for my coffee can prayers and returned to the living room to look through them. God had answered each of them in one way or another—and always on *His* timeline. God had taken a broken woman and made her whole again!

Just then Michael and Lukus walked in. We stayed up late looking at all the handwritten prayers. The lesson for my sons was that they could pray anytime, anywhere. God was always listening. Hopefully they would both grow up to love the Lord as much as I did.

The next morning at church we held hands while singing the final worship song and were bound together in God's love. A wonderful spirit moved through me. It was so strong that I returned the next morning to meditate in a favorite spot of the sanctuary.

After walking up the spiral staircase to the balcony, I sat down in front of the stained-glass window that had taken my breath away from the very first day I saw it. I felt the warmth of the sun, which also painted a pretty rainbow on the red carpet. My once-turned-upside-down life was now full of blessings—too many to count. Just then came the delicate sound of the piano. God whispered, *You are mine*. I hummed while as the familiar lyrics by David Haas came to mind: *Come and follow me. I will bring you home. I love you, and you are mine.*

God had brought me back home where I belonged. A quiet moment followed. What had allowed my spiritual growth? The busyness of life as a single mom or the quiet? I experienced both throughout the years in the apartment.

From the balcony I looked down at the cross above the altar and gave thanks. With the help of the church, its pastors, and the loving congregation, Michael, Lukus, and I had survived the challenges of divorce and we became stronger together!

Later at home, I looked again at the two pictures on the hallway wall, which told a story of their own: our family portrait taken at the church and a homemade Methodist flame plaque that Michael had made in shop class. In that moment I realized the love for my boys and God was infinite and always would be. The best was yet to come.

CHAPTER 9

Hope for a Melancholy Heart

*The fear of the Lord is the beginning of wisdom,
and knowledge of the Holy One is understanding.*
—Proverbs 9:10

"Fear, he is a liar."
—Zach Williams

The sign on the door says, "Stay a while," at a nifty little coffee shop on the town square. The barista hands me a couple of cups of freshly brewed caramel pecan coffee, and I join my friend, who is sitting by the window, where all the seasons can be observed throughout the year. We catch up on the latest small talk. She's witness to the strong woman I have become, having seen virtually every tear and every triumph.

Over four years Charlotte and I had become the best of friends. We shopped for all things bling and met for lunch often. On one outing we stopped at Java since she wondered who was making me smile, and I wanted to show her. Lee was a Christian man from southern Kansas who met us at the shop. He had a touch of an accent, although he said he didn't. I was falling in love with him.

After a year of dating, Lee proposed. Family and close friends gathered at the United Methodist church for an intimate wedding at seven o'clock in the evening. Michael and Lukus wore matching bow ties as they escorted me down the aisle and stood beside us as Lee and I exchanged vows by candlelight. After a short reception, we returned home to start a new life together.

What better wedding gift than a larger home? The apartment was too small for a family of four. A 3,000-square-foot house was on the market three blocks away. We knew it was ours the moment we stepped inside.

The century-old Craftsman house was immaculate and boasted beautifully restored woodwork throughout. The extra space in the basement was a bonus. It would accommodate all our needs, and it had every amenity on each of its three floors. Plus, it included a newly renovated kitchen with a cute breakfast nook—a cozy homework hangout. Out the back door was a patio, a fenced yard, and a garage with plenty of parking space for two teenage drivers.

Moving went smoothly. New living room furniture was delivered and we also bought two oversized recliners in a paisley print for the sitting room, made into a prayer room, which had a fireplace and built-in bookshelves for our collection of Christian reads. On the wall we hung a stunning portrait of Christ.

Michael and Lukus had the top floor to themselves, each with his own bedroom. What a marvelous view of the neighborhood from their rooms! After they were finished unpacking, they helped me shuffle boxes around the house over the weekend, but by Monday I was left home alone to finish, which became overwhelming as the weeks passed.

I dearly missed the simplicity of the apartment, which wasn't lonely like this big house. Besides, keeping the house tidy was going to be a challenge, and it seemed as though the anxiety returned overnight after having been dormant for years.

As my thoughts swirled around all this one day, I was rescued when the phone rang.

Charlotte and I put on our pretties, loaded up in her Cadillac, and chatted while riding the highway. I truly appreciated her encouragement and friendship. We spent hours hopping from store to store and acted like teenage girls as we tried on sunglasses and silk scarves, finally making our way to the designer bags.

I held one up while looking at the price tag. "Charlotte, I love this one, but I just can't."

"Oh, darling—you *must!*" she said. "Treat yourself, Kristi. You deserve it."

She was right, and Charlotte always made me feel special during outings. Good thing this one wasn't over yet! After lunch we looked around the mall and then received pedicures at the salon for the final stop. It was easy to lose track of time. Almost eight hours had passed by. I had not noticed that Lee had called numerous times.

As I walked through the door, he greeted me with a scowl. "Where were you? Why were you spending money?" And so on. Really, what was all the fuss about? I sighed and went straight to the bedroom to unload the shopping bags.

Lee was somewhat controlling. He didn't want any people coming into the house, and it seemed he didn't like my leaving with friends either. But I had really needed to get out. Why not become more involved at church? Helping others helped *me*—why couldn't Lee understand that?

But maybe I didn't understand *his* loneliness. Lee had few friends in town and seldom visited the ones he had in Kansas, which wore on his heart as did the passing of his parents years before. Every night after supper he sat in his chair and didn't utter a single word. I had no idea how to help *his* melancholy heart.

Lee and I didn't go out much together either, other than an occasional Saturday when we drove out of town to browse at a thrift store. At times I would mingle a little too long, and he was silent all the way home, which set the evening up for failure. We spent the rest of the day bickering on opposite sides of the living room.

Sunday mornings were supposed to be cheerful, but that wasn't the case in our house. Every week I shuffled through the walk-in closet and stood in front of the mirror. The reflection caused an abrupt shift in mood. Why did mirrors have to be so cruel? How had I gotten so fat again?

"Aren't you ready yet?" Lee asked.

Being rushed made the anxiety worse, but I managed to find a wrinkled black dress on the floor in the closet and raced to the bathroom for two minutes of makeup. "Fat and ugly, fat and ugly, fat and ugly!" I chanted.

Lee sighed. "Would you stop? You look fine. Quit being bipolar!"

That last sentence could have caused World War III. Why did it always have to be about the bipolar disorder? I grabbed my purse and rushed out the door. Lee insulted me out of frustration while walking to church and didn't stop even as we walked through the doors. How could he?

As we sat in the pew he mumbled words under his breath, which made me sob so badly that I hid my face with my bulletin. In moments like these I silently begged God to take the bipolar disorder away. Just then the pastor's eyes and mine met for a split second—a glimmer of relief since he knew of my struggles. The tears kept falling throughout the service.

After the benediction Lee left in a hurry, but I stayed in the sanctuary, where a friend, Kate, comforted me. She leaned in for a hug and whispered, "I really wanted to lift you up during the time of joys and concerns because I saw you crying, but I wasn't sure if I should."

She was just as beautiful outside as she was inside—and a strong Christian woman. Kate was one of very few church members who knew of bipolar disorder. She *really* understood the struggle, having a close friend with it. Her sentiments were honest and true, and she reminded me of my godly worth and the importance of walking by faith—such words of life in the midst of chaos. There was no better time for me to put on the armor of God to get through the coming days and the upcoming winter.

Snow piled up outside. The dark, overcast days were spent at home for days as I sat on the couch watching reruns. The depression returned with a vengeance, especially after I had gained so much weight. I bought an expensive recumbent bike and used it for a week, but it quickly became a coat and clothing rack instead. Physically and mentally defeated, I started falling away from God. But also in these times I begged Him for mania, which never came.

Thankfully, Charlotte invited me to her house one day soon. A cup of coffee always helped, especially while I sipped it in her sunroom, which was decorated with plants and cozy chairs. She was so easy to talk to and quickly noticed the shift in my mood, just as Mother had years ago. I didn't like *that* Kristi Kay.

Charlotte shared stories about her life and reminded me that some of the things I was dealing with had nothing to do with mental illness but rather issues of being a wife and also a busy mom of two teenagers. Charlotte's words were reassuring and loving, and I was blessed by her friendship although she was thirty years older.

One afternoon I lay back in the recliner all the while mindlessly scrolling on social media and came across a concert announcement. Casting Crowns was headlining in the city! The band was also one of Lee's favorites, and he secretly bought four tickets and left them on the breakfast nook for me the next day with a love note and a Hershey's chocolate bar. It was a thoughtful gift. Maybe he really did love me.

The concert took place in an auditorium in the city. Zach Williams warmed up the crowd with his opening music, an outstanding performance, especially when he sang his new single.

While listening to the words *fear* and *liar,* I instinctively closed my eyes and swayed back and forth to the melody. The lyrics were all too familiar. God's presence was overwhelming.

At intermission I sprinted to the merchandise booth, but Michael went to the meet-and-greet line, where Zach Williams autographed his new saddle bag, which made us both grin. He had met someone famous! We then rushed back to the auditorium, since Casting Crowns was about to take the stage.

The energy in the room was unlike anything else we had ever experienced. Standing room only, hands in the air, Christians of all ages praised the Lord. What a sight to see and hear! We sang along to every song, which filled us with hope and love. Later, lead singer Mark Hall gave an endearing message. This was the best family night! Hopefully the unified momentum would continue back at home for good.

We merely blinked and another year passed by. Lukus was still a bookworm and immersed himself in schoolwork since his high school sophomore year was keeping him busy—as did a job at a pizza place. His big brother reigned as a high school senior and demanded independence. Michael was still my free-spirited and headstrong child and did whatever he wanted, and that agitated Lee at times, who demanded respect in his house.

One night they argued and Lee took his car keys. Michael was angry and muddled a few choice words, so Lee kicked him out. Panic set in as Michael ran out the front door to the sidewalk in the dark of night, walking through deep snow in his tennis shoes. No coat, no hat, no gloves, and no money on the coldest night of the year. I was livid at Lee.

I paced back and forth, finally sat down on the couch, and stared out the window. The strong north wind was fierce and the snow was drifting. Lukus sat down and assured me that Michael would make his way home eventually.

Finally, at about one o'clock in the morning, a clunky Bronco pulled up to the house. It was Renni, Michael's buddy. He was glad to accept a little gas money from me as thanks. Inside, it was time for a "mother and son" chat in front of the fireplace. We warmed up and talked long and hard. He was strong-willed, and I respected that. Certainly we could all get along until graduation.

The four of us gathered for a meal. Lee was grumpy from a bad day at work and started complaining. Then he lashed out at Michael, but I defended him as any mother would. Lee stood up and threw his napkin onto the table. "Yeah, take his side. I'm not doing anything wrong. Then suddenly it was about bipolar disorder again as he told me, "Get better or get out!"

Disturbing thoughts came to mind. *I can't be alone again. I can't get divorced again. What would people think? Where would I live? And the boys? Don't rock the boat. There's too much to lose.*

I started crying and shaking, falling to the floor and rocking back and forth. It was a horrible feeling, and I hated moments like these. Sadness. Despair. Self-hate.

"Just give her a minute, Lee. She's having a panic attack." said Lukus. Both boys sat on the floor and put their arms around me firmly, knowing that the gentle pressure was calming. They had learned a lot throughout the years.

Our bonding angered Lee. "I don't care what she's having—I'm done." he whined while throwing his hands up in the air and walking away.

After the anxiety attack passed, I pleaded with Lee. "Give me another chance. I promise to get help for my bipolar disorder. Let's see a marriage counselor? I'll do anything."

Finding a therapist in the yellow pages was easy. One name rang a bell, and it was that of a Christian clinical psychologist. I had seen her only once in the very early years of treatment, back in 2003, before seeing Dr. Varra. It was amazing how God crossed our paths again for a reason.

Lee and I met with Dr. Ellison weekly for nearly a month. She taught us about the coffee pot theory and conflict resolution. It was up to us to communicate with one another and reduce conflict. During one particular appointment, Lee nonchalantly blamed the marital issues on my bipolar disorder and didn't take ownership for his own negative behaviors. He decided not to return to therapy, which was disappointing. Didn't he want to understand his wife? It opened a new door for me.

Dr. Ellison and I met for individual sessions, primarily to address the bipolar disorder. She could help me identify its *triggers*—a phrase that I was unfamiliar with. She also explained another therapy option, EMDR (eye movement desensitization and reorganization,) which was used to treat PTSD and a myriad of other psychological issues.

The little green rocker became the hope for my melancholy heart. It was a safe place to share all my secrets and the hurt and pain on the inside, which I had carried around for years.

We also tackled distressing events one by one. I could see the lifeless image of my baby and found peace. Reliving the last moment at the house with Derek brought tears. It felt freeing to let go of my emotional baggage once and for all. Then it was time to switch gears and process other predominant issues.

I came to terms with self-mutilation and the body images that had tormented me for years, addressing the fat-and-ugly complex too. In the green rocker a stronger and braver woman emerged, no longer dominated by anxiety and fear. I finally was "rid of the muck," as Dr. Ellison put it. Well, almost. There was one more trauma, one I hadn't spoken about since the Dr. Varra days. I had never been strong enough to talk about it.

I rocked harshly in the chair and felt my heart racing. Dr. Ellison reminded me to relax. Only fragments of the horrible night twenty-nine years earlier fell out of my mouth, followed by a long moment of silence. This was a very private and difficult memory.

As the EMDR session came to an end, relief. Time had naturally healed that wound, and there was no reason to speak of it ever again.

Dr. Ellison reassured me that reliving parts of the trauma was a normal reaction to EMDR and advised me to practice self-care for a few days. How brave I was for facing such a personal demon once and for all!

Processing the trauma brought hope to my melancholy heart. The green rocker was now a place of comfort, healing and *triumph*. The EMDR had cleared the chaos in my head, and tremendous progress had been made! The bipolar triggers seemed to fade away, as did the depression. My strong faith in God played a huge part. My newfound sense of confidence allowed me to enjoy everyday life. This mom was feeling good!

It was a breeze planning Michael's high school graduation. The special day itself was filled with pure joy. Watching him walk across the stage in his cap and gown made me very proud, as did his decision to start a new life. I hugged him for the longest time on the day he ventured to the seclusion of Wyoming, the perfect place for his wild spirit to roam free. But a part of my heart was breaking as he drove away in the old blue sedan. I had given him his wings—it was time for him to fly.

Charlotte and I sat in a cozy booth at the local hot spot and enjoyed their legendary soup and salad bar, plus a serving of bread pudding. "Kristi, I can't believe how calm you are. Thank you for explaining your treatments and sharing your progress. How is your husband handling the new and improved wife?" she asked.

"For the most part, he's been supportive. There aren't as many triggers, so that helps my mood and allows us to get out more. In fact, we just bought concert tickets to see Matthew West." We went on to talk a while longer. Her friendship was priceless. What would I have ever done without her? She always listened intently and gave gentle advice.

Lee and I certainly enjoyed Christian concerts, and we had seen Matt Maher and Casting Crowns twice. Sometimes it seemed that was the only thing holding us together.

The concert venue was packed full. Jordan Feliz opened and gave a stunning performance under the green-and-purple neon lights. When he sang the hit song "Beloved," we felt enveloped in God's love.

The "All In" concert was life-changing. Each of Matthew West's songs had different meanings. My heart was waking up, and God filled my mind, body, and soul with promise. I was exactly where God wanted me to be—and ready to go all in!

After the concert Lee took a photo of me holding a purple concert T-shirt bearing the logo *I am a child of the one true King*, which reminded me of my worth in God. Great things were on the way, and soon came a renewed sense of belonging.

Weeks later, feeling fully confident, I joined the "Grace Team" at church. It was our goal to help members find and use their spiritual gifts. I offered to give another testimony of faith, having served in many other areas of the church. It was my hope to inspire others to use their talents as well. It was amazing how God was directing me toward new things.

Just around the corner in the spring was one of the church's beloved events: the Festival of Tables. It was to be a grand event, and there was much preparation to do.

Charlotte and I loaded up in her Cadillac once again and shopped at Hobby Lobby for all the supplies and decorations. Can you imagine the two of us giggling down the aisles for three and a half hours with overflowing carts? Time passed by so quickly.

"Shine bright like a diamond" The table was covered with a red tablecloth and accented with black, pearls and all things bling—and chicly *over*done. I styled my hair in an updo with a sparkly tiara. The outfit was topped off with a gaudy diamond necklace and flashing ring for fun! Surely that brought a few smiles. The United Methodist Women saw the talented and creative Kristi Kay! This was my forte—the fashionista was still inside! Going home with me at the end of the night was a "Let Your Light Shine" wooden plaque to celebrate newfound confidence.

The next evening when Lee walked through the back door, the look on his face said it all. He was struggling, and he grumbled about his job and coworkers, the interstate, not to mention the crazy idiot drivers that were on it. When I pointed out his negativity, the insults began. "Who do you think you are? You think you know everything?" he said wickedly.

We spent another evening arguing. But this one was the worst. Out of anger, Lee said hateful things, words that could never be taken back—and he grabbed me. In the moment came a flashback. All I could see was Derek and the china hutch. I called Charlotte.

Lee continued muttering, and she heard every word. For once, Kristi wasn't the hysterical one. *I* was healthy. *I* was stable. I couldn't allow anything to risk that.

The next morning I stopped by the church office and talked with Pastor Don, confessing the failing marriage. But what I really wanted was permission to leave Lee. He chose his words carefully and didn't pass judgment or take sides but offered an abundance of prayers for the *both* of us. Hopefully God understood my decision.

Lukus and I went for a drive after school. He already knew what was on my mind, having had a similar conversation with me nine years earlier. I genuinely felt bad for putting him through divorce again. He understood my reasons, which was a sign of maturity. We both agreed to keep it a secret since we hadn't found a place to live yet.

Instinct told me to stop by the old apartment. Surprisingly, there was a "For rent" sign in the front lawn! God's timing was perfect again. The landlord had me sign a lease the very next day. But there was one catch—it wasn't available until fall.

Lukus and I packed and then hid boxes in the basement in fear that Lee would kick us out if he knew the truth. Surely Lukus and I could get through summer and pretend everything was normal. But it was worrisome. A phone call brought good news.

Pastor Eleanor was on the line and extended an invitation to speak at both the Milligan and Fairmont, Nebraska Methodist churches for a testimony series to kick off the summer. The timing was ideal since God was leading me on a new path. There was no better place to prepare than the beautiful sanctuary—there were so many memories.

June came. While I stood at the lectern, the congregation gave me their full attention. I couldn't help but glance at Lee in the front pew. Our five years together flashed before my eyes. How did I find myself in the situation of divorce again? In time, God would bring understanding. Pastor Eleanor's prayer set aside any anxiety.

The testimony of faith included my strong Christian background and the struggles of a single mother. My faith had come full circle since the time I was a young girl, and I mentioned the importance of the poem "Footprints in the Sand." Again, like the dreaming man, God carried me through life's trials.

Being fully immersed in church was crucial because it was a powerful defense from the ugliness of depression. Perfect attendance, singing, praying, taking holy Communion, and putting God first contributed to the strong woman I had become and an unbreakable bond with God. Stepmom Mae was a godly woman and at my worst time she uttered six important words: "You can do *anything* you want." Although she's been gone for many years, I remember exactly how she said it with conviction and love, and I feel her light every single day.

Next I shared parts of one of Pastor Don's sermons that got my attention. He noted that we are not all superheroes. None of us are necessarily extraordinary either. God loves us when we are just ordinary because He made us all special and unique. The sermon had brought me to tears because of my struggles with bipolar disorder. His words had sparked an idea—I had never been anything *but* ordinary. And it was *okay*! God makes us *all* unique, and we all have different strengths. For me, the positive traits of the mood disorder included empathy, creativity, realism, and resilience. Yes, resilience! Besides, all of those things were why I connected so well with music and found strength in contemporary Christian songs heard at church, on the radio, or firsthand at concerts, including the "All In" concert.

In conclusion, I shared one of my own theories—and hoped the congregation would find humor in it: "The 1-800-God Theory." It first came to mind in 2009 while I was speaking with Pastor Eleanor in the sanctuary. She reminded me of the strong connection I had with God. She was right—in the most stressful times, I often made light of the difficult situations and joked that a 1-800 number would be handy. Wouldn't that be so much easier than praying? What if we could all just call up God on our phones and talk to him directly? Well, that might be too easy. We have to have faith!

Speaking brought a world of confidence, and I knew that to be part of the journey. After the service, many people said hello and thanked me for speaking. Particularly, a middle-aged woman and her teenage daughter thanked me for sharing about the depression—it had hit home with them. The girl suffered from it as well. It felt humbling to be a light in the midst of her darkness. That's what it was all about. God and bipolar. My true ministry was yet to be discovered.

When September came, it was time to have a talk with Lee. As we stepped outside to walk to church, the air was halfway between summer and fall and had a crispness to it. The lawns were still green, and an occasional leaf could be found on the ground. When a gentle breeze came out of nowhere, I knew it was God reminding me to trust Him and that everything was going to be okay. Sometimes change is necessary to get to where we are supposed to be.

After lunch with friends, Lee and I returned home to relax in the living room with a cup of coffee. I had to say the words: "Lee, Lukus and I are moving out next month."

He was speechless at first then asked a myriad of questions and wondered if I was having an affair. That hurt. There was nothing left to say.

I worked around the clock—and that's when my magic bipolar superpowers came in handy. Believe it or not, everything was packed and ready to go for the moving service by October. A yellow truck arrived and two men worked efficiently, so much in fact that only one trip was needed for the three-block journey. The short one, with dark hair, scratched his head and asked, "Haven't we moved you before?" We both giggled as I paid him. The rest of the day would be spent unpacking ferociously.

Just after midnight I stared into the bathroom mirror for the longest while. Why were mirrors so important other than revealing who I was *in the moment*? My hair, pulled back in a ponytail, and the dark circles under my eyes showed total exhaustion—mind, body, and spirit. I grasped the cross necklace around my neck and prayed. A half-smile emerged in the midst of tears of sadness and of joy. I was *home*.

CHAPTER 10

Days of Promise

Because of the Lord's great love we are not consumed, for his compassions never fail. They are new every morning; great is your faithfulness.
—Lamentations 3:22–23

"The more I seek you the more I find you."
—Kari Jobe

Walking through the paths of the local tree park, I find peace and inspiration while listening to a favorite band. As I roam up the hills and around the bends, each song tells a story about my spiritual awakening. With each and every step in my life I am becoming closer to God.

The church garden seems like the perfect place to go first thing in the morning, just across the street to the west. The old wooden cross has been taken down and a new white one has replaced it, which matches the garden beds. New plants are emerging through the soil. I too am growing each day and am filled with peace as I bow my head. *Heavenly Father, thank you for another birthday, new beginnings, and bringing me back to the comfort and safety of the apartment. You've brought healing—my mind is clear, and my heart is open. I know you have great plans for me, and I want to serve you more, so please use me where you need me. Prepare my heart for what is to come.*

Every morning after Lukus left for school, I walked a block to swim laps at the community center. It mimicked bilateral stimulation similar to the EMDR. Later, a quick run in the neighborhood with music provided healthy endorphins. Daily exercise was a great defense against cycling from my bipolar disorder.

Weekly therapy continued with Dr. Ellison to deal with feelings related to the divorce. Hopefully the legal process would be quick and easy. My mental health was pristine, and Dr. Elgin noticed and suggested getting out of the house, maybe volunteering somewhere. Even one hour a week would suffice. Meeting new people was a great idea.

The perfect place came to mind—a small museum in the heart of downtown. The curator was middle-aged, dressed casually in baggy jeans and a plaid shirt, and had a delightful demeanor. We hit it off immediately while talking in his tiny office. Roger was excited to hear that I was the daughter of an antique dealer and had a love for visual merchandising. Come to find out, he was an esteemed New York window-dresser back in the day. His portfolio was amazing! It would be quite the honor creating displays together. Who could ever forget the John Wayne poster board? God allowed me to live out a portion of my dream through him.

Then a trendy new consignment shop opened up on Main Street. The bright, colorful awning captured the attention of passersby. The owner was an acquaintance of mine and asked me to be in charge of the window displays. It was too good of an opportunity to pass up. After nearly twenty-five years, God had brought me back to the world of fashion.

Oh, the possibilities! Creativity overflowed! After three hours of picking through racks and blending outfits with accessories, the storefront windows came to life. Customers complimented them, making me feel like a professional all while boosting my confidence. Although I had never made it to New York, I was in smalltown USA living the dream! Plus, it was a great place to spruce up my wardrobe.

Back at church on Sunday I sat in the pew alone, but this time alone wasn't bad. I understood every part of the sermon, and the music was perfect in the moment. After the service, close friends noticed my new dress and the smile that went with it. But they also noticed Lee's absence. It was time to tell them about the divorce. No one ever wants to hear that word, but at least they could pray for us during the process. It was important for me to reassure them that our divorce was not nasty nor bitter and that it was our intention to remain friends.

One of the perks of moving was revamping the apartment, and it was hip and chic. The brand-new charcoal gray sectional was covered with textured pillows with bling and faux fur blankets. In the opposite corner was a comfortable futon on which to kick back and relax. Vases and unique knickknacks that I had collected throughout the years gave the apartment a special touch that reflected a sassy personality.

On the wall I hung an autographed picture of Casting Crowns, and below it was a stack of CDs on the table. I drew a particular strength from *Thrive*, which was a reminder of my spiritual journey, particularly the song "Just Be Held." The lyrics were so inspiring that I had a pendant made with a favorite verse inscribed on it. Wearing it every day was a constant reminder of how far I had come and where my life was going—by golly, it was falling into place. Praising Him kept the bipolar chaos away.

Listening to music on the front porch in the afternoons brought me comfort. The fresh air was nice, and I watched the squirrels chase each other up and down the walnut tree while waiting for Lukus to come home after school. As the cars drove back and forth on the brick street, I pondered where my life was going.

Crown's *The Very Next Thing* CD was brilliant and full of foot-stomping songs. While browsing the official website, I found several books of interest written by lead singer-songwriter Mark Hall. Why not start with *The Very Next Thing* devotional? The subtitle said it all: *Follow God Where You Are. Right Now.* Page 31's list of questions were insightful. What was the bigger picture? Where does God want me?

Hall's writing was so easy to understand and easy to connect with. I could almost hear him speaking in his southern Georgia accent. He had a way with words. Wouldn't it be nice to have a heart-to-heart with him someday?

For six weeks I worked diligently through the devotional book, all the while making notes, meditating, and reading the Bible. My heart began to transform as I realized that my life was really *with* God. My heart yearned for more!

The daybed was a cozy place to curl up with another book, *Life stories*, pausing at the end of each chapter to listen to its featured song. Author Mark Hall describes in detail the stories behind the songs he wrote. For me it blended the love of the Lord with my love of music. The book was informative and touching. Hall's explanations provided me with a strong personal connection.

The song "Set Me Free" was emotional and left me in awe. The story and the lyrics were pleading, powerful, and dramatic. Dark One. Shame. Chains. Free. Jesus. Rescue. The song was so powerful that I played it over and over. Something was really making sense.

Picture me running away from the Dark One in the pitch black as fast as I can, crying out for the Lord. During the darkest times of my life, I was hanging on by a thread and *terrified*.

The bipolar disorder, *my* darkness, had its chains around me. I didn't want to be shackled anymore—only to be rescued and live in the light. *God's mercy saves us.* He was the only one who could truly set me free. Hearing the song brought healing and lifted a burden as I knew that bipolar and God were directly connected. Kristi Kay could finally embrace and accept that there was good within the illness. It wasn't all bad!

Life was simple and smooth. One particular morning, Michael called—he was moving back home from Wyoming. I started a pot of coffee and waited for him to make the long drive home. His arrival at three o'clock in the morning was the best birthday gift a mother could receive.

Although we were tired, we stayed up and had a heart-to-heart. Michael never let anything get him down, even when life didn't treat him kindly. For that I was proud. We always shared a strong spiritual connection. His heart was conflicted. As a mother, the most important thing to do was pray for him. "You pray too, son," I said. His life would fall into place too—someday.

Later in the week Michael caught up with the neighborhood gang while browsing downtown and ran into the beautiful Addie. They had met in high school. She had a heart of gold and was kind to all—truly a rare gem on the inside and out. Addie put a smile on Michael's face, and for that I was grateful. She made his transition back home a little easier.

The charming brick streets were perfect for daily prayer walks. The aroma of autumn was pleasing and the scenery was spectacular—colorful trees in shades of reds, yellows, and oranges, and their leaves dancing to the ground. The squirrels once again provided entertainment as they collected nuts and frolicked around. Simple things brought me joy and contentment.

Why was I noticing so much more? It felt as if my senses were waking up for the first time. Now, everything I saw was bright and vibrant, much better than the shades of gray associated with the dark and depressive episodes of bipolar disorder. Perhaps there was a way to keep them at bay. I was open to what God had in mind.

When asked to assist with the middle school youth group students on Wednesday nights, I hesitated at first in fear of being rejected, as I was a young girl.

A few weeks later an attractive, popular student said, "You're pretty!" But wait—was she talking to me? Her compliment was flattering and gave approval, belonging, and healing to the little Kristi Kay. I agreed to help with the youth group and hoped to help them grow in their faith.

The curriculum included Bible study, artwork, and games. Sharing personal God moments with the students was important, and it was my hope for them to see and *feel* the Light too. At the end of each class we huddled in a circle and put one foot in. An impromptu photo would be a reminder of the different shoes and personalities of the middle school youth group. Then in conclusion we prayed together. They inspired me!

Back at home, Michael, Lukus and I gathered in the crowded kitchen to make a Christmas meal. There was never enough of Grandma Nutzman's ham loaf to go around. And at the table we reminisced and talked about future plans. After dessert the boys left for their father's house to celebrate the holiday with him.

Almost ten years had passed since Derek and I divorced. I looked at my boys every day and saw Derek in them and couldn't help but wonder, *Should we have tried harder?* It was good to remember the love we shared, and time had healed our wounds. Forgiveness was a powerful thing! It was also important for me to pray for Derek despite his feelings toward me. That brought peace of mind.

A blanket of snow sparkled in the moonlight as I stepped outside for fresh air. The sky was dark, and snowflakes poetically fell and gathered onto the red mittens I was wearing, each flake magnificent, beautiful, and wonderfully unique. They're such a gentle reminder from God. I sensed that the New Year would be full of promise.

"Tell Your Heart to Beat Again" played over the radio as I drove to a session of a thirteen-week Christian-based divorce support group. The lyrics and soft piano melody brought me much-needed comfort.

The classroom was filled with middle-aged men and women who had experienced divorce. The sessions were led by certified leaders. The curriculum was simple—we watched a video and discussed various topics, all while making notes in our workbooks. For the second half of class, we broke off into two groups for a more intimate discussion. I had some thoughts to share, having been divorced twice.

After class, participants met at a restaurant downtown for supper and chitchat, which allowed us to get to know each other, sharing about our personal lives, including places of employment. As the night went on, conversation shifted to our faith and the churches we attended. I chimed right in, having served in many areas of the Methodist Church. There was no reason to be ashamed of the life God provided.

On Sunday during worship, Lukus sang beautifully. He sang bass in the school's choir. Lukus looked handsome in his signature specs and dress clothes. He had grown up into a fine young man. I was a proud mother, also because Lukus was an honor student and a prized member of the high school speech team. The congregation knew of his accomplishments, as did the pastor, who caught up with us after service. Pastor Don invited him to serve as a lay reader, assisting during worship service, which would help develop his speaking skills further. Although he was shy, Lukus agreed and later proved to have the gift of articulated speech. As he read the scripture, it brought me extraordinary joy and peace—and I realized God was calling me too! After a service one Sunday, I asked Pastor Don to add me to the lay reader rotation list.

At the lectern one week I had a sense of peace while instinctively looking up at the dove as Pastor Eleanor instructed me to, not realizing that it was for *this* moment. Without God I wouldn't have been standing there.

Pastor Don asked me to be a lay reader again on Easter Sunday, and it made me nervous since the sanctuary would be packed. At home I read the Easter story many times in preparation—and cried each time. My sister was just a phone call away, and her words were reassuring. The Easter story was emotional, and it was okay and appropriate to shed tears while reading it to the congregation. I admired her for touching so many lives as a pastor. Maybe the Lord had something else special in mind for me.

On Easter Sunday the pipe organ was magnificent! Pastor Don and I walked slowly down the aisle and took our places at the lectern. Then after the introduction I read from the Bible the Easter story. I felt important as a leader, and purposeful and blessed. Members complimented me on reading with such emotion. One woman said she felt the Spirit as I spoke. What a beautiful start to this new endeavor! Lay reading was obviously a perfect fit for me.

Back at Divorce Care, strangers became friends. Time healed our wounded hearts. On the last day of class we enjoyed one last meal and fellowship together. Divorce was an ending to the past, but also a new beginning if we wanted it to be.

As I walked out of the restaurant alone, a man in weathered cowboy boots passed by. He tipped his hat and greeted me with a Southern accent: "M'am." He smiled at me in such a way that I realized it had been a long time since Kristi Kay felt pretty. Maybe her heart would beat again someday.

At bedtime that night random thoughts came: *Where will God take me? Who will be in my future?* It was perfectly normal to daydream about a future spouse. But that would be years away, all the while accepting that time alone was mandatory. At that moment

I wrote five things on a bright pink sticky note and placed in it my Bible. All things on the list would bring me closer to God and prepare me for the special man God had for me down the road. There was great contentment in trusting Him with my life—in all areas.

Helping teach Vacation Bible School was very rewarding, and I spent hours creating a fun "Jesus and Beyond" theme. Students of all ages floated through the outer space hallway that led inside a "spaceship" for a week of fun-filled science arts and crafts. I was having a blast, and seeing the kids laughing made me realize why my dad loved teaching so much. At the end of the week I stayed up until two in the morning making an interactive homemade volcano for the final show, at which the kids hooted and hollered to the glory of God.

The church family acknowledged my love for God and service. An opportunity arose for me to lead United Methodist Women Sunday. It was easy following the bulletin, announcing songs, sharing scripture, and welcoming the guest speaker. It seemed appropriate to pay homage to my childhood pastor by reading Numbers 6:24–26 for the benediction. It seemed that life had come full circle, and it all started with Senior Sunday long ago. Things I prayed about for years were coming true! Standing at the lectern felt so natural.

After the service Pastor Don introduced to me some ideas for laity training. Just then a slender woman in her fifties walked past and heard the conversation. She mentioned my obvious love for the Lord, especially while reading from the Bible. Can you imagine the joy I felt in that moment? It brought a world of confidence, and I prayed about it further.

To celebrate, I took a leisurely walk with God! A perfect place came to mind—the nearby park that featured a beautiful flower garden, rich in color and surrounded by a memorial bench. What a grand moment to reflect and give thanks for all the wonderful things God was doing in my life! As I finished praying and opened my eyes, butterflies emerged from the flowers and danced, singing their own song. Only the Lord could bring such love, hope, and joy!

CHAPTER 11

From Darkness to Light

The Lord is my light and my salvation—whom shall I fear?
The Lord is the stronghold of my life—of whom shall I be afraid?
—Psalm 27:1

"Leave it all behind. I have what you need."
—Casting Crowns

Warm days are perfect for lounging outside, so I threw a chunky knit blanket down onto the freshly cut grass in the backyard. There's nothing more relaxing than looking up at the bright blue sky and watching the clouds float by. I simply wonder what it's like up there with Him. As the sunlight peeked through, I whispered, *Lord, help me live in the Light.*

Summer was the best time of the year. I arrived at the pool every day at noon for an hour of lap swimming, not minding if I were the only one there. The guards smiled and asked, "How many miles today, Kristi?"

My daily ritual began by sitting on the edge of the pool with my goggles and favorite swim cap and slipping into the water, then holding the cross pendant in my hand and praying. Each swim is about mind, body, and spirit. *I can do anything in Christ, who strengthens me.*

Swimming under the sun provided the best relief from the anxiety, so much in fact that I took a break from scheduled therapy. But one afternoon I became easily triggered when the pool became crowded and noisy. The young mothers flaunted their perfectly sculpted bodies, wore bikinis and beach hats, and gossiped as they watched their toddlers playing. I couldn't help but look down at my thighs, and out of embarrassment I covered them up quickly with the towel and thought, *When did I get so old?* A downhill spiral started, and over the course of the afternoon my mood shifted as if someone had died. It was time to pack up and go home.

I found myself standing naked in front of the mirror. My old, saggy body was difficult to look at. Overwhelmed by the reflection, I sobbed, *Look at me! I'm just as ugly as I was in school. Those boys were right—I was a dog then, and I still am. My hair is thin and dry. And look at the scars under my eyes. Oh, my gosh—I look like a whale with all this belly fat. Ugh! My thunder thighs will never go away. I hate my thighs. I hate being short and fat. It doesn't matter how much I swim or run. Girl, quit eating. Bump up exercise. God, why can't I just be skinny?*

So I made some changes. Running every morning on an empty stomach allowed me to shed a few pounds. An egg and a shake would suffice for lunch, and then it was off to the pool, where I swam nonstop for hours. Besides, if I stayed in the water I could hide my fat body and shame. Day in and day out the pool was my second home. It was the only thing that helped the anxiety, and there were only a few months to enjoy the sun.

On the last day of pool season, I brought a gift of homemade treats for the guards and staff. While walking out of the locker room, they clapped and cheered, making me feel special, and also revved me up for the final swim, completing for the first time ever a three-mile swim.

I spent the rest of the afternoon lounging in the sun while the music played until the last whistle was blown. The front desk clerk left a note of thanks on my car. I was both happy and sad.

Gone were the days of the lap lane. Gone were the days of gliding through the warm water, the sun, and feeling good. After I returned home, depression set in quickly, and later at bedtime I sneaked into the kitchen and scavenged the leftover brownies. I wanted to throw them up but couldn't.

Returning to therapy with Dr. Ellison was necessary, where we discussed changes in my mood, but I kept quiet about restricting food. My body was pleasingly shrinking and the dark tan disguised the cellulite on my thighs. A round of EMDR could help tame my emotions, but I refused. Maybe next time.

Receiving a call out of the blue from the heart institute was alarming. Two days later a nurse fitted me with a heart monitor for a month-long test. After a cardiologist reviewed it, the results were shocking—I had a second-degree heart blockage and needed a more efficient pacemaker.

Surgery was scheduled immediately. Michael and Lukus took me to the heart hospital, where a dual lead pacemaker was implanted. After the procedure, they headed home. The nurses had me up and walking right away. The other patients, mostly geriatric, noticed my young age. My conversation with them was insightful.

Michael picked me up the next day and drove me straight to the school since Lukus was being honored for homecoming court. We snapped a photo to remember our big moments. Deep down I was sad that it had taken a medical emergency to get us all together. Moments like these fed the depression.

Anxiety numbed every one of my senses. Nothing was wrong. Everything was wrong. I was plagued by throbbing headaches and felt hurt—spiritually, mentally, and physically. I didn't pray or read the Bible. The downhill spiral began.

Lukus was working at the pizza place and Michael lived across town, so the apartment was quiet, and I experienced a new kind of emotional turmoil, an unexplainable void. The girly girl mom missed their laughter, chaos, and messes. What I wouldn't give to go back in time and do it all again! Alone was a very bad place to be.

In an attempt to feel relief, I dug out old totes and looked at thousands of pictures from throughout the years. The sadness was overwhelming. As their mother I couldn't have done better. Why did I have to be the mom with a mental illness? It was hard to deal with. Just then at the bottom of the tote I found a picture of the boys in the sanctuary, reminding me of the promise I had made years ago never to skip church regardless of how bad the depression was.

Sunday morning I took a sulky walk to church. In the pew I kept my head down and didn't bother to sing at all. The hour-long service seemed to last forever. Pastor's words were mumbled from the clutter in my head. I hoped God heard my silent cries: *Why do you abandon me again? Aren't I enough for you?*

After the service Charlotte extended an invitation for lunch and a quick shopping trip to the mall. Maybe next time. The lonely apartment was calling my name.

I quickly pulled away from others and became lazy, lying on the couch all day. It wasn't like me to have a messy apartment. The overthinking settled in at an alarming rate. *You are worthless. You are stupid. No one loves you. No one cares about you. You will never be anyone.* Why couldn't the negativity just stop for one second?

I turned off the Christian radio station and gravitated toward rock music. Some friends called it dark, but to me it was more meaningful, by artists who had mental illnesses too. The songs helped process negative emotions despite what others thought. And no, listening to the darker music did not make me want to kill myself. The *unempathetic world* would.

In the darkness a meaningful song played over and over. It

explained exactly how I was feeling at the moment. How could I ever be fine tomorrow when I wasn't even okay today? I felt the lyrics and they felt me. I was safe for the moment.

On some days music was the only thing that brought comfort. I couldn't just snap out of it or quit being bipolar. But the lyrics of particular artists validated the pain I felt. For that I am grateful, because you know what? We all struggle. And sometimes music softens the blow, and at times it helps me transition out of the dark. But at other times it's a bit harder.

I had another pounding headache, so I lay in bed until noon, skipped a shower, and threw my hair up in a messy bun. While walking to the mailbox, I noticed that the weather was particularly dark and chilly for October—it was just my luck to slip on the ice on the way back inside.

I went straight to the kitchen, opened the fridge door, and stared, then slammed it shut. There was no need for food. Starving myself was a form of punishment. Why couldn't I get down to eighty pounds again? Only I could fail anorexia. In these moments I hid from God.

Feeling defeated and weary, I lay on the floor of the living room and listened to the clock. Tick. Tock. Tick. Tock. Maybe I would just drift off into nothingness forever.

The phone woke me up. Michael was on the line and was frantic since he had blown a tire on the outskirts of town and needed help. There was desperation in his voice, so I changed clothes, put on a dab of makeup, and then drove to where he was on the highway. He rode back to town with me to the tire shop. While we waited, we grabbed a quick bite to eat. I stared at the sandwich and shoved it away.

"Mom, aren't you going to eat?" he asked. "You look skinny and really tired. When did you eat last?" He was concerned.

Silence. Michael was always afraid to ask the inevitable question because he knew *tired* had many meanings. It was more like a *look* that he had seen on my face throughout the years, a stale glare with a frown. Mom was having a hard time again.

Inside I was screaming and wanted to tell him everything, but it wasn't about me. Helping him evened the score. Deep down I still felt guilty for the chaos he and his brother had experienced because of the bipolar, the divorce, and having less. Besides, moms are supposed to be the strong ones.

By the time we returned to the highway, it was nine-thirty and pitch black. I parked behind him so he would have the headlights for changing the tire on the old Buick. Its taillights were bright red and yellow, and they glared on the front of the hood of my car. I felt the car sway from passing traffic. The side of a busy highway was not a safe place to be.

In the silence came whispers from the dark and a familiar cackle: *Come on—you remember me. You've been this close before. Nobody loves you and you're worthless. Come on—all you have to do is step out of the car. All your suffering will be gone forever.*

I was paralyzed with fear. If I did it, Satan would win. I couldn't succumb to his lies, and I cried out, "Lord, help me!" while grasping the steering wheel.

A chill went down my spine, and I looked into the headlights. In that millisecond Michael gazed back at me. My son needed me, and I ran to him, hugged him tightly, and sobbed. As an adult, he could help by listening—and he took care of me in the moment. Parenting had come full circle. After I returned home, God and I had a heart-to-heart—surely I could come up with a plan to *live* with bipolar disorder. It was not going to *kill* me. I had to find balance once and for all. My life depended upon it!

I exposed all my secrets to Dr. Ellison while rocking back and forth in the green rocker. She already knew about the anorexia resurfacing, which had contributed to the downhill spiral. My brain and body needed nourishment. The suicidal ideation was cause for concern too, so Dr. Ellison set up a vigorous treatment plan that included weekly visits and intermittent EMDR. It was the only way. Dr Ellison encouraged me to overcome deep-rooted self-esteem issues and to accept my worth in God. That was a lifelong challenge and difficult to overcome.

In the green rocker, EMDR—we got down to the thick of it all. Not working equaled not being worthy. But also, the stigma of mental illness was distressing. Why couldn't I be normal and live a normal life? The bipolar disorder would never go away, and that was terrifying. Would I make it through life?

Months later as we wrapped up goals and as a part of my healing, I wrote a letter to society and read it out loud during a session. The world had to understand how painful it was to live with bipolar disorder. It was to everyone who had made me feel unworthy and stigmatized by this illness:

A little letter to the rest of the world:

Hey, life really sucks right now. I know I have more than most. I have family who love me. I love my boys. I have an entire circle of friends and I have my church family. I have a nice home and a nice car. I'm happy sometimes. But now, right now, I'm overwhelmed.

There is nothing wrong. Or everything is wrong. I go from happy to sad in a millisecond without any warning. I have triggers. You hit one of those and I'll go down fast. Maybe I was just reminded that I'm not good enough. Maybe I have been reminded I'll never be good enough. That is what Satan tells me all the time. Fat. Ugly. Stupid. Damaged. Worthless.

Sometimes I can't catch my breath. Just for a split second I think about all the times I tried to do it and failed. College with the blades. College and the overdose. The afternoon in the basement when I was first diagnosed, OD'ed again in the house, and the gun incident. And now on the highway.

What more must I go through? I'm exhausted and so tired of feeling inadequate. I want desperately to hear and know that I am loved and I matter. Any ideas for me?

All I really wanted from the world was validation of my pain. Being heard was important. Writing the letter was therapeutic and I didn't have to keep it bottled up on the inside anymore. More thoughts poured out.

Why should anyone have to suffer in silence? Why are we not allowed to share our most intimate thoughts no matter how bad or destructive they are? Why is it so hard to look at someone and say, "I'm really overwhelmed and I'm thinking about ending my life. And right now, I'm choosing *you*. I am literally hanging on by a thread. I'm choosing *you*. Please help me." *Suicide* is a very scary word for the outside world. Even for my own family.

Cries for help are often labeled as attention-seeking, as the smug therapist made me feel years ago. How many times have I thought about ending my life? Fleeting thoughts come and go, but specifically when I'm struggling with triggers during the darkest situations. Think of it as one of the many symptoms of *my* bipolar disorder. At times the fleeting thoughts last for weeks, but other times only a day or even seconds.

With Dr. Ellison's help we can get to the root cause of them. Am I cycling? Am I morbidly depressed? Did something bad happen? If I mention the word *overwhelming*, I *am* having some type of suicidal ideation and am asking for help. Being proactive is half the battle. Understanding I am not crazy is the other half.

Realistically we live in a world that stigmatizes and shames people with mental illnesses. I once read this: "The ignorant are ignorant of their ignorance." Please educate yourselves on mental illness and quit passing judgment. *I am not crazy. I do everything in my power to live a healthy life. This is the way God made me. I will always have a mental illness. Certainly there is a way that I can make others understand.*

While scrolling through social media, I came across a meme that read, "I'm fine. Now read it upside down: "'Help me.'" In the moment it's panic and relief, because that's how I had been feeling for *years*. Maybe someone else would connect with it too, so I posted it on Facebook. Seconds later my phone pinged with frantic messages from my siblings, including a short lecture because it was of sensitive nature, and they knew firsthand of the struggles the bipolar had caused over the years.

I found immeasurable peace and a sense of belonging with its direct meaning, knowing there were others who struggled, bipolar or not. The scrolling continued to find other meaningful and inspirational sayings. Come to find out, there were messages in hidden places.

Just a few days later I received a card in the mail from Opal at church. We met in 2009, and we talked every Sunday. She was gracious, kind, and always had a smile. Opal helped anywhere she was able at church, and she was the very essence of an "old church lady." That's meant with the highest respect. Opal thanked me for being such an active member. She noticed! That was a big thing to a little girl. Kristi Kay was someone! Right then and there I held the card close to my heart and looked up at God. I was worthy! I wanted to be an "old church lady" too. That got me thinking.

I needed to be intentional about seeking Him every day! And I couldn't just go through the motions either. It was time for Kristi Kay to get down to the nitty-gritty and love herself just as God had made her. Then the rest would fall into place. It was time to start sharing my God light with others.

There were simple ways. For instance, sharing a Bible verse on social media or an inspirational story paired with Christian music on Facebook. Posting a daily prayer, thoughts from a devotional or prayer book. A heart emoji can do wonders for the soul!

Each day consisted of a prayer walk. One day in particular, I made my way through the paths of the local arboretum. God's presence and nature went hand in hand. For the first time I posted a video to social media. In the background were trees, shrubs, and the park's majestic beauty, all while sharing lyrics from Third Day's "Offering" and the song's meaning, and even offering to pray for those watching. The Holy Spirit gave me the strength and courage to speak. Kristi Kay was evolving in many ways from the inside out. What a triumph!

I found a sense of belonging in all areas of my life, particularly the church, whether it was lay reading, greeting, assisting, teaching VBS, or helping serve a meal after a funeral. At the store downtown I embraced God-given talents and took pride in my "windows of art." Volunteering was necessary and brought extraordinary healing. All the pieces to the equation were making sense.

I fully embraced the new role of mother of adult children, realizing that we were now friends. At the table we gathered for a casual meal and talked openly about life—and noticed how different the conversations were. I was very proud of the young men I had raised, no matter what the paths they took. They were on their own journeys through life. How wonderful to hear them say, "I love you, Mom," and not needing anything back from them.

Financially I was blessed to have all my needs met and even managed to put some money away. I beamed when Michael and Lukus needed a little help, whether it was giving them a twenty-dollar bill, buying them groceries, or shopping for a new shirt. That reminded me of my father and the first Christmas in the apartment. It's the love you give without expecting anything back!

In therapy I shared a new revelation with Dr. Ellison. The bipolar disorder could be managed. But each day had to start and end with God. During the day I mastered the art of balancing daily life, particularly exercise, diet, self-care, time alone, and time with others. *Weekly* therapy for the past twenty years has been mandatory.

The best defense against the bipolar disorder itself is self-love, reading the Bible, and meditation. All of these nourished my soul, and in the moment I realized that the most beautiful thoughts came from *Him*. My mantra was *Maybe seeing the world through bipolar eyes was the greatest gift God could ever give me!* I finally had understanding and true self-acceptance.

To celebrate, Charlotte and I went on one of our all-day shopping trips. At one store we looked through racks of dresses—and the perfect one chose me! It was elegant, chic, romantic, sophisticated, classy, glamorous, and vintage-like, all rolled into one.

I pranced out of the dressing room and stood in front of mirrors at every angle. Every single thing that made Kristi Kay was standing right there! And it had nothing to do with the dress but the girl inside. It was time to *shine* in the light!

Later we stopped at a fine restaurant for supper to celebrate our friendship. Years of memories come to mind—the lattes, the pedicures, all the conversations, the giggles and tears—the memories could be another book in itself! Charlotte never asked me for anything in return, just to be myself in the midst of my delightfully chaotic life.

Friendship came full circle too. It was my turn to take care of her. God blessed us with love, compassion, and the laughter from our many excursions, particularly the night we drove off into the sunset wearing our scarves and cat's-eye sunglasses. Oh, how I love Charlotte!

Every facet of my life seemed to come full circle. I was baptized as an infant in the Methodist church and later immersed in the water as an adult—and spiritually mature enough to understand its meaning right then and there, surrendering again, giving my life fully to God.

It was then that I started *shining* in the light, and the Christian song "Step by Step" had a more spiritual meaning. It was no coincidence that through the years I had heard it at just the right times—and for the first time on the *very* day the boys and I returned to church in August 2009 while standing next to Dad. Remember? My dad taught me that nothing in God's world happens by mistake. That reminded me of the promise of Romans 8:28.

While I've written at my desk, Christian music always played in the background, especially music by Casting Crowns. The song "Here's My Heart, Lord" once played over and over while I listened to specific lyrics. The words were powerful! *Truth. Follow. Speak. True. Found. Yours. Loved. Pure. Life. Breathe. Healed. Free.* The lyrics spoke of what was on my mind at the moment and it felt as if God had reached down and touched my heart. Literally, *God had reached down and touched my heart.* There was other explanation, and I wept instantly. God also had *healed* part of my heart as well. There was no reason to pretend or be afraid anymore, and there was no more stigma. The pain it caused could be let go for good. I didn't have to pretend anymore.

I no longer had to ask God two important questions: Why did you give me the bipolar disorder? Why did you allow me to suffer in the darkness? I took a photo to remember the moment. The tears were not out of sorrow, only tears of joy and acceptance. God had made me exactly the way He wanted.

A few days later I stopped at a chapel and walked up the steps to the balcony, where I always felt at peace. Maybe I felt closer to God up high, or perhaps just looking down at the altar was comforting. The view was breathtaking! Moments later I sat down in the old wooden pew and played a very special song dear to my heart, "And Now My Lifesong Sings." I repeated the lyrics ever so softly. Oh, how I loved the phrase *lifesong.*

From my personal Dictaphone as I was experiencing this moment I shared these thoughts:

> I'm in the chapel in the balcony looking down at the beautiful stained glass windows. Light is shining through—beautiful magnificent light. In the house of God there is no darkness—only light. Living with God, I will always be in the light. And in the light there is hope. And in the light there is peace. And in the light there is healing—physical, emotional, and spiritual healing in the light. The only way for me to make it in the world with bipolar disorder is with God!

Tears flowed from my eyes as I just then realized a different perspective. While the sun shone through the blue stained glass windows, I envisioned myself stepping into heaven's light. My earthly journey was preparing me for the day when He would call me *home*. Repeat: the day He would call me *home*. I came into the world as Kristi Kay and I would leave as Kristi Kay—nothing less, nothing more. And at that moment in the chapel, I looked up to God and whispered, "I'm free!" His love was overwhelming and always would be, no matter what other circumstances I would face from that moment on.

This brings me back to the here and now, in my cozy office. The walls are covered in pictures from throughout my life, many of which I have written about in this very book. God has never once left my side.

I sit at the desk, which is still delightfully cluttered with sticky notes, knickknacks, and a half-eaten jelly donut. The little girl with the muffin hairdo smiles back at me and I can't help but remember the life she's had. All she's ever wanted to do was belong. But then I realized, I always have. My name is Kristi Kay. I *am* a child of God.

This is a moment of celebration! God calls us all to be brave and share our light with the world, starting right here and right now. As music plays, Kristi Kay raises her hands in praise and dances to the glory of God.

Testimonies of Faith

Note to readers: I have always had a strong faith in God and have been honored to give testimonies of faith throughout the years for various occasions. They are listed below:

- Senior Sunday, 1991, Syracuse (NE) United Methodist Church
- Extravagant Generosity, 2010, York (NE) First United Methodist Church
- Grace Team, 2017, York (NE) First United Methodist Church
- Summer Kick-off Series, 2018 Exeter (NE) and Milligan (NE) United Methodist churches

Songspiration

Songspiration is a collection of contemporary Christian songs that have inspired me. Each had a special message during the ups and downs over the past twenty years.

- "The Air I Breathe," by Michael W. Smith
- "Who Am I," by Casting Crowns.
- "Unbroken Praise," by Matt Redman
- "The Middle," by Casting Crowns
- "The River," by Meredith Andrews
- "He Is," by Mark Schultz
- "Offering," by Third Day
- "The Motions," by Matthew West
- "Just Be Held," by Casting Crowns
- "Beloved," by Jordan Feliz
- "I Will Follow," by Chris Tomlin
- "Worn," by Tenth Avenue North
- "Tell Your Heart to Beat Again," by Danny Gokey
- "All Things New," by Sidewalk Prophets
- "Weary Traveler," by Jordan St. Syr
- "Word of God Speak," by Mercy Me
- "Wonderful, Merciful Savior," by Selah
- "Praise You in This Storm," by Casting Crowns
- "Love Has Come," by Mark Schutlz
- "The More I Seek You," by Kari Jobe
- "Truth Be Told," by Matthew West

- "Scars," by I Am They
- "How Can I Keep From Singing," by Chris Tomlin
- "Oh, Lord, You're Beautiful," by Keith Green
- "The Well," by Casting Crowns

Acknowledgments

First and foremost, I thank God. Without His love and guidance, I wouldn't have been able to find the faith and confidence to complete this book. Every single word has been prayed upon. It is my hope as a Christian woman that sharing my story candidly will help others, particularly those who have been diagnosed with mental illness, along with their family and loved ones.

A heartfelt thank-you to the patients whom I met over the years in the hospitals, in support groups, and in every other way God chose to bring our paths together, if only for a moment. You brought hope, which is why I decided to write this book. Together we must fight the stigma that we face every day. May you all have the courage to share your story if God calls you to.

I thank my father for strong Christian upbringing and for a lifetime of godly encouragement. He taught me always to have faith in God, to speak truthfully, and to stand up for what I believed in. Dad always had the right words, no matter what I was going through, especially after the diagnosis and the years thereafter. I read the prologue to him, and although he didn't read the entire manuscript, I know this book was a project he was proud of, and I know he's smiling from heaven. He knew I would finish when the time was right.

Thank you to my mom, who also believed in a strong Christian upbringing. Thank you also, Mom, for your emotional support the past year. Sometimes we have to be tough.

Thank you to my sister, Cindi, and brother, Craig, who have witnessed many of the ups and downs. I know the drama that comes with mental illness hasn't been easy for you the past twenty years. Thank you for not giving up on me. I hope this book gives you understanding on a more personal level.

To my sons C. Michael and Z. Lukus whom I love with all my heart, being your mother is my *greatest* joy in life. Growing up in the midst of bipolar disorder was challenging and you didn't always understand the how's and whys. Thank you for supporting me in every way a child could—wiping my tears, giving hugs, and just having simple conversations. In your young adulthood, thank you for being present during the worst depressive episodes and anxiety attacks and reminding me to breathe. Just going for a drive with the music blaring was all I needed. Thank you for sharing your recipes, your joys and concerns, and for just saying, "I love you." All of these things reminded me to keep going. Maybe the skills you have learned will allow you to help someone else along the way. Empathy is a powerful tool.

Special appreciation and in loving memory of childhood Pastor Marlon, who watched me grow up in Syracuse (NE) United Methodist church and planted the initial seed. His words on Senior Sunday are still deeply embedded in my heart, as is his late wife, Ruby's, advice, who wrote, "Life is a picture—paint it well," on my graduation card. My true ministry has been revealed at last.

I express the deepest gratitude for all of my pastors throughout the years, especially those from the United Methodist Church— Pastors Pat, Art, Tony, and Trudy. Each one of you has been an inspiration to me through conversations and through your sermons. You may not have known it, but I almost always had a pen in my hand while writing notes in the bulletins. Thank you for taking time to visit when I needed to and for your prayers and words of comfort. You all made me feel loved and worthy. Also many thanks to the

Acknowledgments

various chaplains and pastors who were also part of my journey throughout the years.

I give thanks to my church family at York (NE) First United Methodist Church. You embraced the boys and me in 2009 and have been loving us ever since. Your friendships have been cherished, especially those with whom I am closer to.

Special thanks to all my sisters in Christ, to the many women who have been an important part of my life, including those from the United Methodist Women, now known as Christian Women's Fellowship. I also want to give thanks to the many church friends who have passed away. Your generosity and kindness will always be remembered.

Thank you, Gwyn, for your friendship and encouragement. You are my behind-the-scenes prayer warrior! I appreciate all our conversations and look forward to more coffee time. Thank you, Sharon—you believed in me from the start of this project. Thank you, Sally, for helping with the formatting and for the chat. Thank you, Natalie, for truly understanding. Thank you to all my friends near and far. I wouldn't be here without you!

Special thanks to my beautiful soul sister and friend Linda. You, my darling, have given me womanly confidence and class and are the girly girl friend I never had. I have cherished every moment! God brought us together for a reason, and thank you for listening and for the coffee even when I stayed a little too long.

Colene, I am so blessed that we met in college and have continued our friendship throughout our busy lives. It's not about how much we see each other but the moments that count! You know every single story! And I couldn't have done it without you.

Thank you, dear friends, whom I love with all my heart! You know who you are, and it's impossible to name all of you. If you said a prayer, lifted me up, texted me, greeted me in church, wished me luck, bought me a coffee, hugged me—wherever God put us together—thank you. I am blessed to have so many friends and acquaintances. We are all here to help each other!

Thank you to all my doctors, therapists, and psychiatric providers since the diagnosis in 2003. For José, my first psychologist, thank you for the reminder that *I* am not bipolar, that it is merely a diagnosis. I finally wrote the book! I told you I would. The advice you gave years ago was paramount to my journey.

Special recognition to my treating psychologist for the past five years to the present. You have brought clinical healing for mental illness and constantly reminded me of my worth in God, even when I cry. You kept me going through the most difficult times. I am forever grateful that our paths crossed once again.

Thank you to all the contemporary Christian artists who bring hope to the world, particularly my favorite band, Casting Crowns. Your music speaks to me as none other does. "Praise You in This Storm" has been my life story. And Mark Hall—your words brought me to life. I have enjoyed many books and concerts throughout the years.

About the Author

Kristi was born, was raised, and has lived in Nebraska her entire life. She was baptized and confirmed in the United Methodist Church and has been a lifelong member. Kristi has served as a lay reader, assistant, teacher, and as a member of the Christian Women's Fellowship group. She has also served on numerous committees within the local church and looks forward to new opportunities.

Kristi has two adult children who live in the same community. She enjoys spending time with them, which includes swapping recipes and cooking.

She enjoys listening to all genres of music and watching movies. Kristi enjoys exercise of any kind, especially distance swimming, running, Pilates, and spending time at the gym chasing natural endorphins. She welcomes a walk or coffee with a friend anytime.

In 2003 Kristi was first diagnosed with bipolar disorder, and shortly thereafter she decided to write a book. The first draft was titled *Understand Me*. For many years her writing went dormant, but she continued collecting notes and thoughts throughout the years until 2009, when her writing began again. But the daily struggles of her bipolar disorder, raising children, and everyday life thwarted her attempts until 2021. Kristi always believed the project would be completed on God's timeline.

On March 17, 2023, Kristi celebrated twenty years with the diagnosis of bipolar disorder and is living a healthy and stable life. During the completion of this book she experienced a life-changing event but persevered with God's guidance and knew it to be part of the journey.

Her treatment plan includes weekly therapy and medication management. Kristi also practices numerous alternative therapies, including massage, neurofeedback, cranial electro stimuli, and herbal sauna tent and massage, all of which help manage the bipolar disorder. Kristi has not had an inpatient hospitalization since January 2006 and attributes that to her strong faith in God and acceptance of her illness. Peer support is of utmost importance.

Kristi sees herself as an advocate for those suffering with mental illness, and she plans to follow where God leads in this respect. She encourages anyone who is considering suicide to call 988 or to visit *988lifeline.org*. Please remember that you are *not* alone. There is always hope.

Parting Thoughts

God uses broken pieces. For God, broken pieces are not put in the trash. He mends them together one by one until they're made whole. God is the one who created you; therefore, no matter how you feel or what you've been through that made you broken, He can mold you back into your best piece. You are God's masterpiece.
—Anonymous